Books by Howard Moss

New Selected Poems

Howard Moss

New Selected Poems

New York Atheneum 1985

NOTE: The poems are reprinted in the sequence in which they originally appeared within each book with two exceptions: "More Lives of the Great Composers" was first published in *Rules of Sleep*. On reflection, it seemed more fitting to place it among the poems selected from *A Swim Off the Rocks*. "Einstein's Bathrobe" was not the final poem of *Rules of Sleep* but has been shifted in position to become the last poem in this book.

Poems from the following previously published books are included in this volume:

THE WOUND AND THE WEATHER: copyright 1946 by Howard Moss; copyright renewed 1974

THE TOY FAIR: copyright 1946, 1947, 1948, 1949, 1950, 1951, 1952, 1953, 1954 by Howard Moss

A SWIMMER IN THE AIR: copyright © 1957 by Howard Moss

A WINTER COME, A SUMMER GONE: copyright © 1960 by Howard Moss

FINDING THEM LOST: copyright © 1965 by Howard Moss

SECOND NATURE: copyright © 1965, 1966, 1967, 1968 by Howard Moss

SELECTED POEMS: copyright © 1969, 1970, 1971 by Howard Moss

BURIED CITY: copyright © 1975 by Howard Moss

A SWIM OFF THE ROCKS: copyright © 1976 by Howard Moss

NOTES FROM THE CASTLE: copyright © 1979 by Howard Moss

RULES OF SLEEP: copyright © 1984 by Howard Moss

For Harry Ford

Contents

A Winter Come, A Summer Gone (1960)

Finding Them Lost (1965)

Second Nature (1968)

New Poems (1971)

Buried City (1975)

A Swim Off the Rocks (1976)

Notes from the Castle (1980)

Rules of Sleep (1984)

From The Wound and the
Weather *(1946)*

Clichés for Piano and Orchestra

For Peter Brooks

1

That accidental morning
No garden could deny
Pleasure its misuses;
Cicadas cried bitterly
The language of their briefness.
Then, in the wet eye,
A hopeful desert shook
Its windward, dear oasis,
But I, with a backward look,
Ran from the dread seducers.

2

If I had come to kiss
Cinderella on the bank,
I would know more of this.
I hovered on the brink,
Twirling parent images;
Then, as my heart sank,
The sun sank in the rushes.
I played my water wrist
As a fisherman a line,
But it fell, it fell, all the way down.

3

Plants cannot travel,
Water cannot speak;
The green leaf is rooted,
The blue lake is mute.
(O dark in the dark.)
But if love is a miracle
And I may marvel,
Last night when I woke,
Plants knew distance
And the water spoke.

4

By the shore-line talk
Of the fresh-water lake,
And the rubbery kiss
In the underwater dark,
By the clutched hair there,
The blue swimmer's lips
Coming near, I swear,
Though the autumn is here,
That the summer took
What it could not take.

5

If trial and error knew
How little in the end
Matters the true blue
Or the defying, false friend,
How thin the line between
Matter and then none,
The body and the mind,
The grass and the stone,
Then will would be simple
And one decision ample.

6

As the statue came alive
In the catastrophic purple,
I dug my grave
In the name of the people;
I wrestled with the stone
Till I had no name.
The statue ruled awhile,
Till I struck it down;
Then I could retrieve
My flesh and bone.

7
Relatives and friends,
A coffin is our end.
Our silhouettes grow thin
When the worm gets in.
(Black is the bed of green.)
Tie to your skeleton
Therefore your name;
When the wind harps on it
And you are naked to sun,
I will be as you. We will be as one.

Waterwall Blues

I gnarled me where the spinster tree
Unwound its green hosanna
And built its sorrow, leaf by knee,
A lachrymal cabana.

The selfsame night I cracked my cowl,
Unwound myself with Anna;
Speech by speech and howl by howl
O don't you cry Susanna.

I left my childhood sadness near
The winder of blue water,
Walking in the windmill year
With his summer daughter.

That very night I spoke my piece,
Unwound my heigh-ho merry;
Started my newfangledness
Across her downtown ferry.

But when my halfway laughing gulls
Despair the death of her,
Dumb sorrow rides the same old hulls
With his mad mariner.

Around the Fish: After Paul Klee

The mind from nature, divorced by love,
Stunned into being by the running wave,
Swims backward always. Around the fish,
Unreasoning sensation made a wish.
Parsley, persevering in a tree,
Maturely withers in the alchemy
Of elms and willows. So with us
The elementary is most serious.

2

Wishing, the Fisher King sat down
(Bait was his body, but his catch a crown!)
Incarnate fish food rose again,
Hooked to the level of his flawless line;
The sea stirred; sunlight's mica hurled
Aroma of the fish around the world;
Darwin breathed it on another shore,
Gasping the less than liquid air.

3

Swimmers, crying in the undertow,
A water blinds us where we go;
The whirlpool of the inner eye
Has wet ambitions, casts its fly
On sightless water; baited, fed,
Its fishing pole hangs by a thread.
But Christ lies on the blue plate, still.
The spawnless salmon strike to kill!

From The Toy Fair *(1954)*

Venice

Its wingéd lion stands up straight to hide
The source of pain: the reign of the unnatural.
One cannot tell how really false the real is.
One cannot tell how real the really false is.
Seen in one light, we apprehend the Beautiful:
The thinnest minarets of lattice lacework
Tangibly recovered from the hardest natural
Elements command our endless homage:
One doorway makes our human lives seem trivial.
In yet another light, a scabrous limb of Venus,
Dangling in rank water, rots to golden bone—
The swank and stink of the imagination
Beautifully gone bad. Its waterways re-weave
The only city that has seen itself
Reflected in the mirror of its very eye,
Made-up, each century, in vain for views
No one can now remember. How the painters lie,
Taken altogether, in their fabrication!
Even the Adriatic, static in its green,
Evokes no known sea. From the campanile,
One sees, face down, a short, ceramic fish
Glittering its red-tiled scales below.
Exquisite emphases and subtle losses
Make up its tide. For power, four bronze horses,
Brought from Byzantium, outpace the sun.
Dwindling to our shadows in outside salons
Where orchestras of afternoon rehearse our evening,
We sound the very history of fear we felt
Through all the shorter histories of fear we feel.
Is it true, we think, our sorry otherness
Is to fall in love with beasts whose beauty ruins us?
Those beasts are everywhere, though Venice says
Lions to be golden must be painted gold.

The Lie

Some bloodied sea-bird's hovering decay
Assails us where we lie, and lie
To make that symbol go away,
To mock the true north of the eye.
But lie to me, lie next to me;
The world is an infirmity.

Too much of sun's been said, too much
Of sea, and of the lover's touch,
Whole volumes that old men debauch.
But we, at the sea's edge curled,
Hurl back their bloody world.
Lie to me, lie next to me,

For there is nothing here to see
But the mirror of ourselves, the day,
Clear with the odors of the sea.
Lie to me. And lie to me.

A Balcony with Birds

The mind drowned in the sun may dream of birds
    All downed, too heavy to arise, but when
The trees release their shuttlecocks of wings,
    Which bank of birds is but imaginings?
The eye must follow form, but from this height,
    I see how softly summer parries weight
Till everything alive weighs less and less
    And, thinly felt, the weighted consciousness,

No thicker than green leaves, or the meridian,
    Grows thinner, even, to absorb the sun.
All heaviness goes up, and up the clouds—
    Those thin patricians thick as Roman crowds
Assumpted in white togas into blue—
    Yet painful in the light, the real, in view,
Drifts back to the roof and the ailanthus tree—
    Fern of impermanence, but heavenly.

The light that hangs in the ailanthus weaves
    The leaves' leavetaking overtaking leaves.
The actual is real and not imagined—still,
    The eye, so learned in disenchantment, sees
Two trees at once, this one of summer's will,
    And winter's one, when no bird will assail
The skyline's hyaline transparencies,
    Emptying its architecture by degrees.

Roundly in its fury, soon, the sun,
    Feverish with light, goes down, and on
Come ambitious stars—the stars that were
    But this morning dimmed. Somewhere a slow
Piano scales the summits of the air
    And disappears, and dark descends, and though
The birds turn off their songs now light is gone,
    The mind drowned in the dark may dream them on.

Burning Love Letters

1

Fire that cancels all that is
Devours paper and pen,
And makes of the heart's histories
A cold hearth warm again.
It could as well consume a branch,
Blank paper or black coal
That now, in ashy avalanche,
Scatters the heart whole.

2

What words led to the end of words?
Coldly, all separate sighs
Shiver in flame, flying upwards,
Merged into burnt lies.
In somersaults of light, words burn
To nothingness, then roll
In dead scrolls, delicate as fern,
Or hiss like a waterfall.

3

From partial feast to total fast,
From object to mirage,
An animal that cannot last
Appears in fire's cage:
Love's crazy dog in a cold sweat,
Far from its neighborhood,
Circles the puzzle of regret,
On fire in the wood.

4
Love's ashes lie and will not rise
As fire dies to a black sun
And makes of the heart's histories
A warm hearth cold again.
Cremation's scattered dust confronts
Dead vision, and in these
Ashes I write your name once,
Bending on cold knees.

A Lesson from Van Gogh

Speechless tree and animal and bird
Vein dreams with meaning, often blurred—
If we could but connect the beast and word!

Unharmed by guilt or will, day after day,
The silly fish, performing in the bay,
The simple serpent, lion, pig, and jay,

Are not more separate in each other's sight
Than we who speak—our speech engraves the night
With all the hieroglyphics of delight

That daylight cannot translate. "Take my ear,"
One painter said, who painted out his fear.
Madness has a poetry that comes too near

Truth for comfort: though the mind goes numb,
Thinking of that severance, the deaf and dumb
Communicate by signs, and everyone

Can follow the plain meaning: "Talk to me,"
Van Gogh was saying, "I am not a tree,
A fish, a serpent, lion, pig, or jay."

Winter's End

Once in a wood at winter's end,
The withered sun, becoming young,
Turned the white silence into sound:
Bird after bird rose up in song.
The skeletons of snow-blocked trees
Linked thinning shadows here and there,
And those made mummy by the freeze
Spangled their mirrors on cold air.
Whether they moved—perhaps they spun,
Caught in a new but known delight—
Was hard to tell, since shade and sun
Mingled to hear the birds recite.
No body of this sound I saw,
So glassed and shining was the world
That swung on a sun-and-ice seesaw
And fought to have its leaves unfurled.
Hanging its harvest in between
Two worlds, one lost, one yet to come,
The wood's remoteness, like a drum,
Beat the oncoming season in.
Then every snow bird on white wings
Became its tropic counterpart,
And, in a renaissance of rings,
I saw the heart of summer start.

The Hermit

Always there is someone who has turned away
From the important mornings and the evening's eye,
Who sits on the top of a tall stairway
Somewhere in the country, or at the edge of slums,
And lives there quietly, day after day,
And does not turn his head to look our way.

What made him leave our ashes and our love?
Did the open sky above the city tempt
His ragged senses to the green, unkempt,
Free countryside? And now to disappoint him
The leaves are shy, and the fractious birds
Dither about their nests and songs.

Loving the mountains, hating the shore,
Wherever he is, he is not far
From whatever it is that brought him there.
Left in a circle of deserted air,
He draws the edges round him like a tent to hide
The wanderer, traveling inside.

His eyes are wild, his island is insane,
We say, and envy secretly his deeper calm.
He calls it home. Perhaps inverted pride,
Pursued in childhood, was his suicide;
Or maybe once, walking in a crowd,
He shuddered at the passion at his side.

Dressed for a battle that has taken place,
Or will never happen, he masks his face
Against the hostile, preferring the alone.
Tuning his armor to the distant guns,
He writes, in a circle, on his shield:
O *miseries and appetites of the world.*

Adolescent's Song

Lopsided love in hotel rooms,
And desperate love, asleep in tombs,
And hour-glass brides and mock bridegrooms,
Are not the pure friends that once were we,
O Timothy, Timothy, Timothy.

The mirror man and the paramour,
And broken glass on the slanting floor,
And the midnight punk and the drunken whore,
Are not the pure friends that once were we,
O Timothy, Timothy, Timothy.

The vacant loves in apartment halls,
And boys for boys and girls for girls,
And the wilted love that pays the bills,
Are not the pure friends that once were we,
O Timothy, Timothy, Timothy. ,

Goodbye. Bon soir. Farewell. So long.
The singer is parted from his song.
To whom should the singer's song be sung?
Not the pure friend that once you were,
Timothy.

Mountain and Clouds

Does the hand of God
Sign the accord of cloud?
I see the formal hills
Run with abandoned light,
One out of two worlds made
By the algebra of night.
Does the scene shift by itself,
The green take, shelf by gulf,
Its evening net and spill
All drama on a hill?
Slapdash, a splash of light,
On moored, chromatic dark,
Invites the eyelid's tight
Enclosure to a park
Where everything is green,
Or everything is dark,
Or even the dark is green.

All traffic on a tape
Winds uphill and down.
(I see abandoned hills
Still in a formal light.)
Invention spoils it all:
We cannot leave alone
Contraptions of the will—
While ruins we create
Clog the mountain gaps,
The cartographer of cloud
Magnificently maps.
The visible reveals
Invisible mystery;
And the hand of God is green,
If it is the hand of God;
If it moves at all, it moves
According to a cloud.

Elegy for My Father

Father, whom I murdered every night but one,
That one, when your death murdered me,
Your body waits within the wasting sod.
Clutching at the straw-face of your God,
Do you remember me, your morbid son,
Curled in a death, all motive unbegun,
Continuum of flesh, who never thought to be
The mourning mirror of your potency?

All you had battled for the nightmare took
Away, as dropping from your eyes, the sea-
Salt tears, with messages that none could read,
Impotent, pellucid, were the final seeds
You sowed. Above you, the white night nurse shook
His head, and moaning on the moods of luck,
We knew the double-dealing enemy:
From pain you suffered, pain had set you free.

Down from the ceiling, father, circles came:
Angels, perhaps, to bear your soul away.
But tasting the persisting salt of pain,
I think my tears created them, though in vain,
Like yours, they fell. All losses link: the same
Creature marred us both to stake his claim.
Shutting my eyelids, barring night and day,
I saw, and see, your body borne away.

Two months dead, I wrestle with your name
Whose separate letters make a paltry sum
That is not you. If still you harbor mine,
Think of the house we had in summertime,
When in the sea-light every early game
Was played with love, and if death's waters came,
You'd rescue me. How I would take you from,
Now, if I could, its whirling vacuum.

From A Swimmer in the Air

(1957)

A Summer Gone

For Mildred Wood

1

The brilliant seaside glitters its farewell
To bathers who pack up their stripes and go
Home from all the cottages that water built;
Deserted on deserted dunes, those stilts
Of slipshod timber watch the sun run out
Among their crooked legs to meet the sea.
The windows, darker as the days go by,
Drink in the liquor of the autumn light.

2

The spiral shells, now empty of their hosts
That noiselessly would hunt the sands at night,
Are not more empty than a house I know
Whose windows, boarded up, are black with dark.
The inner and the outer night converge
On blind astronomers who used to search
The summer sky for stars. The stars that fall,
In quick succession, are not seen at all.

3

Intrinsic as the crickets are to night,
The summer night is music made by them.
Uncritical, we listen to their themes.
The little orchestras that lure the stars
Down, down from fiery perimeters,
Until we seem to touch them with our hands,
Have chirped into a silence. Where are they
Who plucked the hours of our sleep away?

4

Is it love that makes our summers shine?
Ideas of love, I mean. The naked limbs:
Bronze gears that cut the bluest sky to shreds
By running past reclining, sandy heads?
Sweet breasts that hold the very heart of love?
All shapely weights that we are mad to love?
Those beautiful outsides, those thin-skinned maps
Are part of love. Or all of it, perhaps.

5

The insects scatter on their flimsy wings
And disappear. Sometimes you find a trace
Of one, and see a wingless carapace
Erosion has a mind to sculpture in.
They are such tiny fans, such bits of skin
You cannot hold them in your hand. The wind
Will bear, invisible upon the air,
Those cenotaphs to nothingness away.

6

Sea purses lie on the September beach,
Miniature, old-fashioned sleds of black,
The runners clawlike, paired parentheses.
These are egg cases of the skate or shark,
And if they ever held their dangerous young,
Indented by the hand, like dry seaweed,
The horny little shapes hold nothing now.
Each is an artifact that you can hold.

7
There is a time when feeling knows two things:
The dead bird lying, and the whir of wings.
Those travelers who beat the upper air
Have clarities in mind—a south somewhere,
Where clouds are higher and the sea more blue.
Diviners of the tropics have to go
Where summer is still spoken. Autumn wings
Time the distances between two things.

8
Sad fall, a thousand dyings color you:
The sunburnt skin of leaves. Of love, the view
To take is but another wintry one,
To wait for the new nestings of the sun.
Happy for the leaves that make us sad,
We walk across your fields of richest plaid,
Grateful for the view. We'll have, someday,
That other weather that we salt away.

Underwood

From the thin slats of the Venetian blinds
The sun has plucked a sudden metaphor:
A harp of light, reflected on the floor,
Disorients the chair and desk and door.
Those much too delicate hands still tapping
The Underwood seem now Hindu dancers
Or five or ten young Balinese children
Hopping up and down in a clearing where
The striped light scrapes through bamboo seedlings
And moves from skinny shade to thin veneer
And changes as the harp of light is changing
Its twanging image on the office floor,
Being so remarkably the blinding heir
Of something that is not, and yet is, there.

Once I watched at the water cooler
A face bent over the jet-thin water:
The iris of the bent eye changed its color
As if the water jet had stained it green;
I saw the animal head's slight shudder
Lifted from the surface of that running stream.
Tall branches then grew green in the hallway,
Arching above a green-ferned pathway;
A screen of green leaves hung in the doorway.
Was that a mirror where I saw the beaked birds,
The sluggish coffin of the alligator,
The monkeys climbing up the sunlit tree trunks?
Or did distortion, in that corridor,
Create, like the harp, its sudden metaphor?

Inside that drawer, among the blotters, folders,
Memos, carbons, pencils, papers,
Is the youngest animal of all awaking
In that coarse nest where he's been sleeping?
If I should reach into that dangerous drawer,
What singular teeth might pierce my skin?
Or if he should leap, should I then kill him,
And watch, where the harp had set its lightness,
The marvelous animal blood go thin?

A Swimmer in the Air

That sea we see of surfaces
Turned upside down would be another world:
A bone shop, soaked in pearl, a dumping-
Ground for rarities, the sea-maws pumping
　　Grecian garbage Roman cities hurled
　　Seaward westward toward our faces.

That sea would yield up secret farms,
　　Gray-rotted by itself, encrusted thick
With unimaginable wealth, the spoil
Of deaf-mute drownings, the immemorial
　　Dead, floating in a blue-green bailiwick
　　Of nun-like plants waving arms.

That sea will not turn over. See
In its deepest keep, far from its shallow,
The formal, hidden iceberg, slant, oblique
With pregnancy below, thrust up its peak—
　　Like ourselves in the water-beasted wallow,
　　Caught in a cellular ecstasy.

In the same vein, all flesh conceals
Articulation's fishnet, whose thread-bones
(A metaphysic harp from sky to heel)
Hang in the flesh that dangles from the creel
　　Depending from the weedy Hand that owns
　　All fishnets and all fishing reels.

His answers breed a further question:
The fingernails of scale a snake will shed
In spring, coil after coil, on moistened clay,
Though similar to the serpent wriggling away,
　　Are but facsimiles, though not quite dead.
　　Testing this, see how the rest shun

Drying memorials to that race
That mined our viewpoint in the Garden,
Whose inching tape maneuvred in the sun
To measure every guilty length of Eden.
　Man is an animal that needs a warden
　　To frighten off the Master's face,

　　For even an idiot sees a world
　No tree or dog would dream of, finds a name
For pain or absence of it, marries love
Of one kind or another. In his grove,
　Insensible fruit trees and wild game
　　Grow naturally, though he lies curled,

　　The spit and image of our wish,
　Smoking a pipe, with an ice-cold Cola
Clutched in one hand, and the Sunday funnies spread
On both his knees. He'll leave his lurching bed
　To throw hot jazz on an old victrola—
　　A far cry from the primal fish

　　Whose fine-boned spine our back remembers:
　The river bottoms, and the sea-silt soft
As soup, the mudflats where night crawlers came,
Tempted by the water tops to change the lame
　Arrangements, making of the air a loft
　　Fitted to our brackish members,

　　And out we clambered, eyeing land,
　Our moist eyes focused on the moron green,
Hot on our backs abnormal dryness, shadow
Forming in the seanets, seaweed into meadow,
　Finally landing at the foot of pine,
　　Heavy with salty contraband

While the birds beautifully beat blue
On erect wings, as magically they soared,
Feathered and efficient, from tallest trees to stake
A claim so ravishing that now we undertake
To map an area we once ignored,
Still exiles from that upper view,

For, mummers of the ocean's Word,
Our dry translations tidied from the deep,
Bespeak its ancient languages. The salt
Our tears and blood must harbor from its vault
Is shed on every beach-head where we creep,
Part man, dry fish, and wingless bird.

The Falls of Love

1

I know so many stories marred by love,
Tales told by bitter voices in the dark:
Those who stand before the open window
Afraid to see their hands that might let go;
And other hands that count departed loves,
Ten icicles inside a pair of gloves.

2

What faces tell its crooked narrative
Make everywhere their small appearances:
Dried flags of warning that commemorate
A feast that failed, or fasts that failure fed;
Or worse, young faces that too soon reveal
How eyes may witness what they cannot feel.

3

Only lovers rest in summer's grove,
Warm in the hollow belly of the hill.
They feel the lizard's slowness, see the sea
The mother of desire, and become the tree
They shelter under. As those leaves of skin
Burn, they burn to say: Love, stay, till autumn.

4

A winter comes where love will never live:
In darkened windows, shadowed heads receive
Night sounds that hold affection in their strings,
And harp on the harpings of themselves to give
Cold strumming warm illusion, and to stir
False, five-fold music in the listener.

5

A body without love is in its grave.
There is a still life that all sleepers dread
That only love can motion from the dead.
Though he walk upright where green grasses wave,
He wears a little earth upon his head
Who shuns the marriage for the single bed.

6

They rise up shining who have love to give;
Who give love freely may all things receive.
Though streams they cross can never be the same,
They know the waters of the earth are one;
They see the waking face inside the dream
Who know the variations are the theme.

7

I know so many stories marred by love,
What faces tell its crooked narrative.
Only lovers rest in summer's grove;
A winter comes where love will never live.
A body without love is in its grave—
They rise up shining who have love to give.

Those Who Cannot Are Condemned

*Those who cannot remember the past are condemned
to repeat it.*   SANTAYANA

Shipwrecked in daylight and docked in dark,
The blindman lacks a mirror in each eye,
But from the ticking clock and the crowing cock
He maps, in the dark, a visionary sky.
Seeing all the planets and the stars plain
Inside his head, and sensing the terrain,
He needs no walking stick to walk again.

No repetitions dawn, no dusk comes back,
Distinguishing the twilight from the sun,
And though his world is uniformly black,
Sometimes he sees its forms in unison.
And there are those who see far less than he
Though seeing more, and choose a twisted key
To lock themselves from their necessity.

For memory distorts the ghosts that ply
The glassy lightness of their mirrors; they
Tempt the senses to a kind of play
In which the characters are scenery;
No audience awaits the end but one
Who stares at nothing and will blindly run
Equally from midnight as from sun.

Some closet all their dead behind one door
And mourn the apparitions they have sown
And rattle on the knob while they implore
Freedom from a jail, which is their own.
Some ageless children murder dreams they gave
Away too soon, and harpies in the grave
Make merrier the birth-rites while they rave.

And some invent a calendar that time
Has never witnessed, drawing on the air
Impossible mythologies, and some
Drag through the Odysseys of their despair,
And locked up, finally, in self-made doom,
Wander in their night from room to room,
Unweaving threads of their unsubtle loom.

And some rehearse a future that the world
Will weed out carelessly: uprooted trees
Flung in a field, and from the first imperilled
By hunger, war, color, or disease,
And others, in great pain, will travel far
For false translations of the way they were,
And some will die not knowing who they are.

The Gift to be Simple

Breathing something German at the end,
Which no one understood, he died, a friend,
   Or so he meant to be, to all of us.
   Only the stars defined his radius;
His life, restricted to a wooden house,
Was in his head. He saw a fledgling fall.
   Two times he tried to nest it, but it fell
   Once more, and died; he wandered home again—
   We save so plain a story for great men.
      An angel in ill-fitting sweaters,
      Writing children naive letters,
   A violin player lacking vanities,
   A giant wit among the homilies—
We have no parallel to that immense
      Intelligence.

But if he were remembered for the Bomb,
As some may well remember him, such a tomb,
   For one who hated violence and ceremony
   Equally, would be a wasted irony.
He flew to formal heavens from his perch,
A scientist become his own research,
   And even if the flames were never gold
   That lapped his body to an ash gone cold,
   Even if his death no trumpets tolled,
      There is enough of myth inside the truth
      To make a monument to fit him with;
   And since the universe is in a jar,
   There is no weeping where his heavens are,
And I would remember, now the world is less,
      His gentleness.

Letter to an Imaginary Brazil

For Elizabeth Bishop

The pink tongues of certain flowers having
Only colloquial names (they are
So tough they might be used for scouring)
Stick out suggestively among green pods,
And the green's tough, too, though it surprises
The fingernail that frees its milk from fibre,
Running a white thread down the hand. One plant's
No menace, but from the plane, one sees
A writhing settlement that hides its danger,
Where snake and puma wrestle on a floor
Of sliding vegetation, and the macaw
May tear a scale off as loud and brilliant
As any virtuoso bending over keys
Of black and white—those colors missing here,
Where all is earth-green, earth-red, earth-brown,
And a sulphurous yellow takes the breath
Away from the breather, Elizabeth.

The waterfall, cruel as a kind of love,
Which, because it moves, is forced to cut
Some life away, is still a version of
The pastoral by being beautiful:
A dynamo that distance turns to song.
The mountain, too, has its deception—
Imagined stillness, though explorers lie
Ironed out among its dark crevasses,
Where nature tries to wrest its forms from darkness:
Twisting, thickening spines and circles
Frightening the mind with a naturalism
That cannot weigh the difference between
A feather and a leaf. To fall asleep at night,
One thinks of nature as a human being:
The mountain a patriarch bending over life,
The waterfall a girl, stranded in a myth,
Whose tears have cut through rock, Elizabeth.

38

Though what is still may move, and come to grief,
Though what is moving stop, no longer safe,
I see you in your house upon a mountainside,
Lighting the lamps. When you look outside,
There is the room, hung up between the mountains,
Reflected on the other side of glass,
And, swinging in that double cage of light,
The mind flies out to objects of its love
And finds impenetrable forms and shapes
That you can formulate when you pin down
Each butterfly of thought upon your board.
You'll see, as fine as fern, a single tree
Which, sprouting all its foliage at once,
Will seem to move beneath a microscope
Until each cell is separate to the eye,
Thin-scaled as life upon the width of death,
Who cannot read your poems, Elizabeth.

Local Places

The song you sang you will not sing again,
Floating in the spring to all your local places,
Lured by archaic senses to the wood
To watch the frog jump from the mossy rock,
To listen to the stream's small talk at dark,
Or to feel the springy pine-floor where you walk—
If your green secrecies were such as these,
The mystery is now in other trees.

If, in the desert, where the cactus dryly,
Leniently allows its classic bloom
To perfume aridness, you searched for water,
And saw, at night, the scalp of sand begin
To ripple like the sea, as though the moon
Had tides to time those waves of light's illusion,
The rock that spilled so softly from your hand
Is now ten thousand other grains of sand.

If you lay down beside the breathing ocean,
Whose lung is never still, whose motion pulls
A night-net over sleep, you knew the way
It lulled the dreamer toward his vision, how
Drowned mariners turned over in its slough,
Green-eyed among the weeds. You see it now
A less than visionary sea, and feel
Only its blue surfaces were ever real.

Or if you were born to naked flatness
Of rock, or rock that twisted up in mountains,
The jagged risers stonily ascending,
And bent down once to see the mica's tight,
Flat scales of silver, layered in the granite,
And kept one scale to be your jewel at night,
Another sliver now breaks light; its gleam
Is similar to yours, yet not the same.

Once history has used your single name,
Your face is one time will not see again.
Into such a din is every singer born,
The general music mutes the single horn.
The lights in the small houses, one by one,
Go out, foundations topple slowly down—
The tree, the sand, the water, and the stone,
What songs they sing they always sing again.

Tragedy

Does a tear fall from the eye
When, falling from great heights,
The body usurps the sky
To die of its appetites?
Do the limbs seek the land
And the lungs a last song
When, burned by cruel wind,
They hurtle headlong?

When to that center hurled,
Kings have far to fall—
So high, they see the world
Smooth as a round ball—
Perspective takes their wit,
And sceptre, crown, and ring
Must somersault to it,
The whole world darkening.

Those falls from pinnacles
Through miles of royal air
Turn widely in their wheels—
Beggar and priest are there.
All flights of steps may lead
To terror at the top,
The heart begin to bleed
Suddenly without stop,

As when old Caesar's whore
Tore Egypt from her skull,
Or Hamlet's Elsinore
Broke for a lack of will,
Or King Lear on his heath
Invoked the end of breath,
And fools fell out of myth
Into a real death.

All saviors of the city
Are lit by an unknown star;
Love, terror, pity
Walk where they are.
The kings of our great ills
Are dead, yet come to mind
When we fall from small hills
Into the common ground.

A Winter Come

1

When frost moves fast and gardens lose their ground
And gold goes downward in the trees, no sound
Accompanies departures of the leaves,
Except when the wind hurtles into air
Dead shapes the coming winter will inter;
Then the thinnest music starts to stir
A faint, crisp scraping in the startled ear:
The leaves that feed the new leaves of next year.

2

A child lay down in his imagined grave
To see the form he'd make engraved in snow,
But even that feigned hollow filled with snow,
And, rising on a landscape blurred a bit
By shadows of an adumbrated blue,
He came upon two worlds he had not known:
One was his being, one his mind let go
Until the light would take the blue from snow.

3

Your breath precedes you on a winter's day,
An insubstantial cloud, as if to say,
All solid things are blown to vapor soon.
Look up! The scimitar of the moon
Is but a remnant of the round it was,
Is but a ringlet of the ring to be,
As, riding forth, the breath that marked your birth
Will have its heir, before it comes to death.

4
As birds come nearer for a crust of bread
Across the frozen snow, by hunger led
To stamp fine footprints on a scroll of white,
So winter is a world where appetite
Grows bolder by necessity, where the fox
Betrays his fable, and the cold unlocks
Stiff beggars from the doorways. Time grows old
In the knuckles of an old man blue with cold.

5
The racing waterfall that slowed in fall
Has thinned to a trickle or an icicle
And stands as quiet as the rocks it willed
To move. As though expecting it to fall,
A listener stands upon a rim of silence,
Seeing a changed world prepared to change,
The waterfall silent on its breakneck shelf,
And silence a spectacle in itself.

6
Those statues, born long after funerals
Have mourned their subjects, stand in every park—
Stone statesmen, stiff upon their pedestals,
Who dominate indifferent day and dark.
Blind to all the cruder jokes of snow,
A socket of sheer cold behind each eye,
They cannot know that even sculptors go
Where all the celebrated sitters lie.

7
And what of love that old men dead and gone
Have wintered through, and written messages
In snow so travelers, who come too warm
To what may grow too cold, be safe from harm?
They know the fire of flesh is winter's cheat
And how the icy wind makes young blood sweet
In joining joy, which age can never have.
And that is what all old men know of love.

8
Who reads by starlight knows what fire is,
The end of words, and how its mysteries
Go running in the flame too quick to see,
As language has a light too bright to be
Mere fact or fiction. By ambiguity
We make of flame a word that flame can burn,
And of love a stillness, though the world can turn
On its moment, and be still. Or turn and turn.

From A Winter Come,
A Summer Gone *(1960)*

King Midas

My food was pallid till I heard it ring
Against fine china. Every blessèd thing
I touch becomes a work of art that baits
Its goldsmith's appetite: My bread's too rich,
My butter much too golden, and my meat
A nugget on my plate, as cold as ice;
Fresh water in my throat turns precious there
Where every drop becomes a millionaire.

My hands leak gold into the flower's mouth,
Whose lips in tiers of rigid foliage
Make false what flowers are supposed to be.
I did not know I loved their warring thorns
Until they flowered into spikes so hard
My blood made obdurate the rose's stem.
My God was generous. But when I bleed,
It clogs the rosebed and cements the seed.

My dog was truly witty while he breathed.
I saw the tiny hairs upon his skin
Grow like a lion's into golden down.
I plucked them by the handfuls off of him,
And, now he is pure profit, my sculpturing
Might make a King go mad, for it was I
Who made those lively muscles stiffly pose—
This jaundice is relentless, and it grows.

I hate the glint of stars, the shine of wheat,
And when I walk, the tracings of my feet
Are affluent and litter where I go
With money that I sweat. I bank the slow
Gold-leaf of everything and, in my park,
A darkness shimmers that is not the dark,
A daylight glitters that is not the day—
All things are much less darling gilt this way.

Princess, come no closer; my tempered kiss,
Though it is royal still, will make you this
Or that kind of a statue. And my Queen,
Be armed against this gold paralysis,
Or you will starve and thinly bed alone
And, when you dream, a gold mine in your brain
Will have both eyes release their golden ore
And cry for tears they could not cry before.

I would be nothing but the dirt made loud,
A clay that ripples with the worm, decay
In ripeness of the weeds, a timid sun,
Or oppositely be entirely cloud,
Absolved of matter, dissolving in the rain.
Before gold kills me as it kills all men,
Dear Dionysus, give me back again
Ten fingertips that leave the world alone.

2 THE QUEEN'S SONG

The palace clocks are stiff as coats of mail.
Time stopped; he flicked it with his fingernail.
O he was mine before he was a mine
           Of gold.

Time's twelve cold sentinels so grimly still
No longer chime their golden interval.
O he was love before he was the love
     Of gold.

What treasurer is this, come to my bed,
Whose suppleness is now a golden rod?
O he was King before he was the King
     Of gold.

3 THE PRINCESS' SPEECH

I praise the bird, the river, and the tree.
One flies, one flows, and one has made me see
That, standing still, the world is turning me.

I cannot fly. Birds carry in the morn.
I cannot flow. A river bed is born.
I grow. My leaves are green, and gold, and torn.

Divided into two, I am a tree.
The branches are too high for me to see,
The roots too hidden from reality.

They say that veins of gold lie underground.
Beware, explorers, of the spoil you find:
Though you sail back and forth, you sail around.

The laurel grows upon the laurel tree.
Apollo plucked the string of mystery
And made a golden echo in the sea.

4 THE QUEEN'S SPEECH

May every child of mine be barren, golden!
May every beast become a golden swine!
Here is a list, O gardeners and huntsmen,
Of what to kill and what to leave alone:
All natural things must go excepting those
That are by nature golden. Whatever grows
The King's touchy color let live, but close
Your nets upon the pink and crimson rose.

But I will save one rose tree in this pot
That I may gaze at it, and when he's not
About, I'll look and look till light is gone
At flower, petal, stem, and leaf. And then,
I'll ponder how a King became a fool!
Long live King Midas! And the Golden Rule!

5 THE HUNTSMAN'S SONG, THE GARDENER'S REFRAIN

Is it the hawk or hare,
Blindly alive to feed,
The daylight rises for?
I have seen both bleed,
Yellow and dead.

Is it the clang of war
I waken to instead
Of the hunt as heretofore?
That shot was in my head,
Yellow and dead.

The quarry goes before.
The hunter must be fed.
I know the huntsman's lore.
I know that blood is red,
Yellow and dead.

Nature cannot bear
To gild its marriage bed
With gold that is not there.
The golden goose is dead,
Yellow and dead.

6 ADDRESS BY DIONYSUS

There is no meekness in my sun.
It is more dazzling than the one
You cannot look at, Midas. Run
    This way or that, it follows you,
    And is indifferent to the view.

A king especially must live
Without a God's prerogative.
We take, for every gift we give,
    Two back. Your gold made you a fool.
    Now you grow wise, but in my school.

There is a lesson children learn:
You reach your hand out, and you burn.
It is no lesson kings can spurn.
    Mine is a cruel curriculum
    Not fit for the powerless or dumb.

Go to the river. Dip your hand
Into its silver rumblings. Stand
Still while the precious contraband
　　You glitter with flows from your skin
　　Till water sucks away your sin.

It is through will, and only will,
Pleasure unearths the sensual.
The Gods grind error in a mill
　　Whose gold wheels turn all costly wit
　　Into its dreaded opposite.

7　THE PRINCESS' SONG

See how they love me,
Green leaf, gold grass,
Swearing my blue wrists
Tick and are timeless.

See how it woos me,
Old sea, blue sea,
Curving a half moon
Round to surround me.

See how it wants me,
High sky, blue sky,
Letting the light be
Kindled to warm me.

Yet you rebuke me,
O love, love I
Only pursue. See
How they love me!

What I loved most most moved me.
Tell me, soul, where now your motion is.
Looking back, I look on Orpheus,
Who, looking back, looked on Eurydice.

His voice is distant as the shelled sea.
She, underground, is where no music is.
They moved me most who loved me.
Tell me, flesh, where now your motion is.

I, an ancient King, walk blindly.
I break on pleasure where no pleasure is.
Looking back, I look on Orpheus,
Who, looking back, looked on Eurydice.

9 DIONYSUS' SONG

Midas in the street
Makes statues out of men.
When man and money meet,
Beware! The worst is then.

Beware! The worst is then.

When animal and angel
Meet on a common ground,
And elegance is natural,
Nothing is so profound.

Nothing is so profound.

My daughter, the river flows down to the sea.
All things begin in its rich nursery.
If you should shed a tear, shed it for me.

Remember me for this: if you should gain
What men most wish for, give it back again,
Before the Gods transform it into pain.

Stay here beside me while I dip my hand
Into the cold river. Until water end,
Pactolus, from this day, runs golden sand.

The Dumb Show

As many as there are of star and root,
One shifting its position underfoot,
One changing its appearance overhead,
The faces hang their flowers on the dead,

Each dreaming: I am not and am this one;
Sometimes I am the moon, sometimes the sun;
Each tunneling a way up from the dark
Where ghostly busybodies, hard at work

At change, are trying on a thousand things:
The graces of the sea, the rush of wings,
The scalings and the seedpods fleshed on time,
Each trembling on the fact that is its name.

Putting on or taking off in sleep
The many-colored coats of Joseph's sheep,
Some wildly alter hem, some pluck at seam,
The lame becoming lions, the lions tame,

Each thinking: What I thought I was I'm not;
I am transformed into the opposite
Of all I seemed to be; I live by strings
Whose ends are fastened onto other beings,

Each making up a kind of makeshift man
Whose tatters are composed, catch as catch can,
Of other selves, now peering out, now in,
Each walking up and down inside his skin;

I feel my heart collapse within its walls,
The humpty dumpty of my ego falls
Into a thousand eggshells of defeat,
For though I hate those strangers when they eat

My heart out, I must also dine on them;
I add their substance to subtract my sum;
I grow into a kind of crippled thing
That cannot crawl or fly or creep or sing

And lies at the bottom of a sandy pit
Where something larger, looking down at it,
Demands its silence. Though it is not me,
Sometimes I think it often tries to be.

If I could only dream myself way up
To the stinging air of freedom at the top,
Rise up from causes I can never reach,
Oh, then, I might say something close to speech.

If You Can

Countryman, tell me if you can,
When your fist rounds the tender corn
And shakes the minerals of the grain,
If one can live by bread alone.

For I have loved

Fisherman, tell me if you can,
When your scarred, glinting catch is slain
And pitted on the rock, if then
The diamonds of the sea are torn.

For I have loved
But not loved well

Physician, tell me if you can,
When you part wires in the skin
And open up the bank of bone,
Is the blood sea or is it sun?

For I have loved
But not loved well
And cannot tell

And you I walk on, if you can,
Tell me if you are snow or moon,
Or rise by some invention
Into a garden out of stone.

For I have loved
But not loved well
If I have loved
At all.

Pine

Its fringy needles stiff
As horsehair, glaucous, fine,
Form a kind of leaf;
Each leaf's a smaller branch,
Each branch a smaller tree,
The whole scaled to the inch,
The inch to infinity.
And so pine is what Plato
Might deem the universal
Universal, for
It is that metaphor
With roots in the divine:
The great in the small design.

A pair of winged seeds—
Each like a butterfly
With wings at the vertical,
Folded, at rest—can fly
Out over the world
And haul up in the sun
The bud and bone of pine.
Ecclesiastical,
Beautiful short or tall,
We cut it down. And yet,
Revenge is in its wit:
When we are cased in it,
There's pine to every fit.

Explorers

Though Circe's music lured Ulysses on,
Less famous instances of silences
Have worked an equal magic: Coming down
Rivers, crossing seas, in desert spaces,
There were a thousand nights when no one spoke
And the stars dipped away in the cold dark.

The weary animals, afraid of wind
On sand, their legs as delicate as grass,
Fed on what vegetation came to hand,
While sailors stoked the ocean's underpass,
Miles away, for treasure or for truth,
And heard the same wind discharge its wrath.

And there was fact and there was magic: trees
That spun around or fought or stood stock-still,
A myth of fishes and a book of leaves,
And setting forth to find the sacred hill,
Where mind and body parted in their dread,
And the left hand dreamt, and the right hand did.

What shores receded as they sighted land!
What bellied sails embarked, splendid of motion,
To lay their wings upon the sea, unmanned
Ambassadors of dry rot to the ocean.
Young tyrants, in a fever, shook with cold,
Before they tumbled down, or else grew old.

And it is all the same. The king, falling,
Rises in new splendor but to fall again;
His jealous princeling, who can kill a king,
Is waiting in the wings, and then walks on,
Yet disputatious arms retake the field
As dead kings sift the layers of the world.

And those who passionately would not see
That time and silence take what they would have,
In fear, or love, have sought the mystery
Of what lay menacing beyond the grave,
As once, in Florida, water would not sing
When Ponce de Leon babbled at the spring.

The Truth About Love

It seems to have traveled mostly at night,
Supremely ironic, lighting fires,
Laying golden eggs in the midst of squalor,
Its outer garments, in the latest version,
Sumptuous, its linens more than shoddy,
Drunk, moreover, at a seedy party
The discriminating shunned, and, later, bawdy
In a run-down neighborhood, with whores and sailors
Chosen as companions while the queen went needy.
Now that everything about it is known,
Why does it come up purple or threadbare,
Thrashing all its sunsets in a fit of pique,
Or stripped, in the seamiest hayloft, ready
To repeat dull anecdotes the millionth time,
Its poise unquestionable, its voice unsteady?
It is brilliant, androgynous, and stultifying
With its threats and tears, dissembling always
Its mad obsession with the blurred distinction.
And yet who else
Is so elementary and badly needed
That fifty cultures rise at the merest rumor
Of its presence, and, finally, punctually fall
Whenever it departs, as if on schedule?
Interviewed, Monday, in the city dump,
Which turned, by magic, into a hotel tower,
Shedding poems and paintings for its bath
(It takes ten centuries of running water
To wash it clean), it then emerged, all dirty
Again, in a costume of ferocious splendor,
A hat some milliner in old Vienna
Sweated over, its pumps exchanged for sneakers,
And raced across the city, breaking records,
Just to prove its powers of endurance.
It lies down anywhere, and loves the country,
But is so unassuming it can even flourish

Beneath electric signs and in railroad stations
It goes to for the summer, estivating,
It says, near fountains that escape our notice,
And comes back in the fall, its ribbons flying,
Wheeling through the leaves, singing all the voices
Of every opera in the repertoire
Plus one no one has ever dreamed of writing.
Going about its gigantic business,
It masks itself as any shape or hope,
Appearing as a vicious telephone call,
Or a flat, disturbing message in an envelope.
It praises calmness but adores upheaval,
Is most to be desired when it apes composure,
And much to be distrusted when it boasts it has
The only fingerprint that can be changed at will.

From Finding Them Lost
(1965)

At the Fire Fountain

(Christmas, Radio City)

The twisted wreath that emulates a crown
Of thorns hangs up its Christ, the blood-red berry;
What blood once ran true scarlet in the vein
Runs now to crooked waste: the inventory
Of all the sudden wealth we get and give.
Yet, the selfsame martyrs still endure
Poverty, the occupation of the poor.

Here, the fountain's question marks of haze
No longer glaze the marble. Winter's spare,
Bone monuments of stone and glass appraise
Themselves across the plaza, the evening air
Holds up the starlight in that silent, queer
Moment of perfection when each thing assays
Its selfhood only, and perception stays.

Diagonal Prometheus, gilded, bare,
Strains his hard gold body and gold hair
To flight that trembles in an abstract fire;
A pine is centered in a tent of wire
Above his head, and as the tongue-tied hour
Breaks upon the bells, the season's martyr
Merges with the vision of the fire-bringer

To burn two parables to one: The rack
Whose nails of fire pierced the hanging Jesus
Blazes as that stone where chained Prometheus
Suffered the vital eagle coming back.
The portents of this night ascend to mourn
Our deaths in theirs; on two crossed sticks, on stone,
By thorn or beak, in anguish, Gods are born.

Water Island

To the memory of a friend,
drowned off Water Island, April, 1960

Finally, from your house, there is no view;
The bay's blind mirror shattered over you
And Patchogue took your body like a log
The wind rolled up to shore. The senseless drowned
Have faces nobody would care to see,
But water loves those gradual erasures
Of flesh and shoreline, greenery and glass,
And you belonged to water, it to you,
Having built, on a hillock, above the bay,
Your house, the bay giving you reason to,
Where now, if seasons still are running straight,
The horseshoe crabs clank armor night and day,
Their couplings far more ancient than the eyes
That watched them from your porch. I saw one once
Whose back was a history of how we live;
Grown onto every inch of plate, except
Where the hinges let it move, were living things,
Barnacles, mussels, water weeds—and one
Blue bit of polished glass, glued there by time:
The origins of art. It carried them
With pride, it seemed, as if endurance only
Matters in the end. Or so I thought.

Skimming traffic lights, starboard and port,
Steer through planted poles that mark the way,
And other lights, across the bay, faint stars
Lining the border of Long Island's shore,
Come on at night, they still come on at night,
Though who can see them now I do not know.
Wild roses, at your back porch, break their blood,
And bud to test surprises of sea air,
And the birds fly over, gliding down to feed
At the two feeding stations you set out with seed,
Or splash themselves in a big bowl of rain
You used to fill with water. Going across
That night, too fast, too dark, no one will know,
Maybe you heard, the last you'll ever hear,
The cry of the savage and endemic gull
Which shakes the blood and always brings to mind
The thought that death, the scavenger, is blind,
Blunders and is stupid, and the end
Comes with ironies so fine the seed
Falters in the marsh and the heron stops
Hunting in the weeds below your landing stairs,
Standing in a stillness that now is yours.

The Upside-Down Man

"I have brooded well,"
Said the Upside-Down Man,
"Measured the interval
Between I will, I can;
My silences are sound
As they die into birth;
My feet are off the ground;
My head is down to earth.

"The footlights of the moon
Shine up on my ten toes
In silvery grit, and soon
A brighter spotlight glows;
At the sun's fire drill,
When the insects all sign off,
They gradually compel
The sounds of birds to life.

"So all my days pass by
In light and in music,
Day's coming a slow sigh,
Night's going far too quick,
For then the moon must wane
And vanish from my leg;
Its change from thick to thin
Is my whole travelogue.

"I've heard of the Other One
Whose balance is as God's;
The tightrope of the sun
Is where he promenades;
His head where his feet should be,
He bares it for a curse;
Sometimes I think I see
My shadow in reverse!

"I've tried a somersault
But am no saltimbanque;
Cartwheeling through cobalt
Made me sick; my heart sank,
My tongue slid round my teeth
And my limbs trembled when,
With one expiring breath,
I aped the Upright Man.

"Yet I foresee the day
When my sky-underground,
Forsaking gravity,
Will turn the world around,
And, standing on my head
(My feet, I think, to you),
Weighted, disquieted,
Lopsided, what I view

"Be terrible: the towers
Sink down through cloud and sky,
The excessive, shy flowers
Uproot themselves and die,
My beloved moon look
Away so it cannot see
How my chained feet work
At time's misery."

The Roof Garden

A nervous hose is dribbling on the tar
This morning on this rooftop where I'm watching you
Move among your sparse, pinchpenny flowers,
Poor metronomes of color one month long
That pull the sun's rays in as best they can
And suck life up from one mere inch of dirt.
There's water in the sky but it won't come down.

Once we counted the skyline's water towers,
Barrels made of shingle, fat and high,
An African village suspended above
The needle hardness of New York that needs
More light than God provides to make it soft,
That needs the water in the water towers
To snake through pipe past all the elevators
To open up in bowls and baths and showers.

Soon our silence will dissolve in talk,
In talk that needs some water and some sun,
Or it will go the same way as before:
Dry repetitions of the ill we bear
Each other, the baited poles of light
Angling through the way the sun today
Fishes among the clouds.

                    Now you are through
Watering geraniums, and now you go
To the roof edge to survey the real estate
Of architectured air—tense forms wrought up,
Torn down, replaced, to be torn down again . . .
So much like us. Your head against the sky
Is topped by a tower clock, blocks away,
Whose two black hands are closing on the hour,
And I look down into the street below,
Rinsed fresh this morning by a water truck,
Down which a girl, perky in high heels,
Clops by, serenely unaware of us,
Of the cables, gas lines, telephone wires,
And water mains, writhing underfoot.

The Silences

1

Now you are back at your window,
Where you live in a strange city,
Now I no longer see you,
Your face is slowly forgotten,

As you are forgetting to watch me,
And I will forget to remember
How lately alike was our wanting,
That wanting which ends in hurting.

Wherever you were, your presence
Still clings to all things in absence;
There is also the pain of touching
What you touched without ever knowing,

And the trees hold the rain in silence
As the rain makes the birds stop singing;
In the sea is a pool where the pressure
Of your body still seems to be moving.

Your body is still and is moving,
As I remove from each mirror
The frost where your face was reflected,
As if coldness could be abstracted.

Silence is pain. You hear it
Most when you cannot bear it.
Tell me if you can bear it,
Far body and near spirit.

2

The air bears nothing on it.
No. But I saw this minute

You slowly move upon it;
Then there was light within it.

I see it now no longer,
That light when late we linger

Upon the shore, the distant
Sun growing less persistent,

The moon being not quite present,
And the stars still evanescent.

3
Trance I have loved so surely,
Surely your naked branches have me,
I who have loved your comely
Body of branches moving toward me.

Nightly to sleep so safely
Even the pang of others' dreaming
Comes over distance faintly,
That is to be less lonely, only

What is there still rearming
The arms I take up in the dark,
The olive branch extending
Into an arrow's pointed ending?

4
Moonlight is half of sleep
And the keepsake of the deep.

I plunge into sleep's sure crater.
Slowly it fills with water.

Your hands that can never reach me,
How all of their labors touch me!

Weeping at their occasions,
The seasons turn the seasons,

A sound not unlike the ocean's.

5
The inward pleasure of water edges
Drifts as the shifting color battens
On dead wood, filling the golden pockets
Of fall with the falling brown detritus
Of unloved leaves as my eyes go searching
For faces among the stain of the going
Wood on an island filled with the samples
Of revived and reviving underpinnings,
Whose death under white fall soon is coming
But to rise up again in greening
Time. And, in time, the dead start growing.

6
Now I am back at my window,
Where I live in a strange city,
Now you no longer see me,
My face is slowly forgotten,

And the trees hold the rain in silence,
As the rain makes the birds stop singing;
My body still seems to be moving
That wanting which ends in hurting.

In the X-Ray Room

Beneath a canopy for which the whole city
Seems, this morning, to be painting stripes,
You splash past a glass door while your taxi
Shifts and is off to a thousand other lives;
In the sudden hush of the jaded lobby,
The mirror sees you walking toward its knives.

Ring and Enter. Entering the waiting
Room, doom says that it's polite, that one
Must face the worst alone in unabating
Silence. The news becomes important. Shun
The pain of others, or in contemplating
Theirs the fear you bare will be your own.

The market falls and rises while a ticker
Tape taps out the bedlam of your wits
In a room as brainy as a shrewd, old broker
Inside whose head a stock quotation sits.
Deserted in a cubicle, you wait and stare
At a blank wall, and smoke two cigarettes.

Invisible grower, gardener of alarms,
You lie on a turning table cold as snow.
Down press the camera's praying-mantis arms,
Avid to embrace your negative below;
Your inner organs light their secret farms
Not even lovers come close enough to know.

Deep in the inner landscape of yourself,
You search for contours that the camera plots;
Each mountain is as dangerous as each gulf.
And now you are rising with the speed of jets
To shatter through black glasswork at the top,
As someone says, "You can get up. Get up."

And if that day should dawn, the gradient blue
Be unexceptionable, the cliché birds
Fly up again to where they always flew,
And all the voices sing of large accords,
Whose lone dissenter will be only you,
What justice will there be in just rewards

That day, if, running for your life, you run
Into the X-ray of the broken straws
Of all your veins, and pain shoots off its gun
For the last time, and the target knows it knows,
When all the miraculous drugs are gone,
The precious weight of everything that goes?

The Fall

Where are you going that I want to go?
You have disappeared where I cannot follow.
There are new ghosts that come by daily.
Evening snow is coming down slowly.

Now I am staying where I always stay,
Between the truth's twilight and the half lie,
Which are the same and not the same, oddly.
Evenly snow is coming down slowly.

Did I ever tell you what I meant to say?
Or was I silent as this snowfall? Was I?
How can I take your sudden darkness lightly?
Heavily snow is coming down slowly.

The world is being shut away now. Surely
You felt what I felt. Lately, early
In the morning you rise up from the earth. Unearthly,
Heavenly snow is coming down slowly.

Crossing the Park

Crossing the park to see a painting
Somebody painted of the park—
One that I once found more enchanting
Than the park itself—I stopped to look

At the cocksure pigeons mincing on gravel,
The trees, each reading its own green book,
And felt the amphibian nerve and muscle
Of life quiver like a tuning fork,

Then steady itself to evoke some distant,
Wordless country existing still,
Growing louder on what was silent,
Its wild, sad energy visible

In hundreds of forms of pulsing shadow
Boned by the light, and then formed again
By the light—to the right, an imperfect meadow,
To the left, a sleeping, unfinished man—

Forms never to be composed so neatly,
Finished, framed, and set out to view
As the painting that hung in the nearby gallery
In permanent green, in abiding blue,

For any vision must mean that something
Is being omitted; being discrete
By making the possible seem like one thing
Means lopping the head off or the feet,

Or leaving a leaf out or one wave
Of that merciless connoisseur, the sea,
Or pretending the body exists for love,
Or forgetting the pictures of misery

That are found in the news each day, that spell
Out fortunes each night across the sky:
The terrible kingdoms of the small,
The crystal ball of every eye.

The sun relinquished the sky. In slow
Inches the shade climbed up the trees.
Too late to get where I started to,
I watched their metamorphoses

Gradually give up the light
Till there was nothing more to give
To leaves and lives whose forms dispute
Those parks, those paintings in which I live.

The Sea to Hart Crane

"Enter me carefully for
Deeper than poems I change;
My scansion, shore to shore,
Stretches beyond your range.

"You'll find no bridges here.
Those Orphean strings you pluck
Will strangle you on a dare.
The wet nurse that you suck

"Nourishes nothing but
Cold blood, cold weed, and strange
White buildings. And what you put
Awry, I re-arrange.

"Music drowns in the dark-
er music that I alone
Can play. But first the shark
Will rend you bone from bone,

"And my skill is so fine,
I grind the dreadnought
Down to a hairline
On the shell of purest thought."

Lu

When the flower got caught in webbing
And primness stained her sensuousness,
The clarity of alcohol gave repose,
A false repose that led to guilt,
And soon guilt's little meandering mandate
Sped to a maze in a black mirror
Where a white flower at the center
Kindled itself in a glassy blur,
Or maybe it was only under water . . .

The heavy afternoons creaked by
Like carts uphill on a cobbled road.
The cure for fear was also fearful.
Staring in a mirror filled with cobwebs,
She turned to the hand that offered help
And bit it—bit it as hard as she could.
Waking from the dream, she tasted blood.

The small humiliations flowered
Into a plant, then into a tree,
And soon an entire nursery
Stretched away as far as the eye could see,
In which, in the center, quite alone,
She stood to hear the general mockery—
The cruel applause of a crowd at a bullfight
Where either way praise has a victim.
But sometimes she
Could hear the distant battery
Of a radio deflected by the tile
Of the four walls of a swimming pool,
In which, at the bottom, the flower lay.
And there was echo, echo, echo—
The tears that fell inside her head
So endlessly, so silently
That, almost recognizing finally,
She thought she heard.

She took to doing inappropriate things,
A bland and ludicrous tragedy,
Like fainting at Altman's, bleeding at Schrafft's—
She could think of no other scenery
(The Greeks eluding her and pleasure being
All that there was to Italy).

Soon, everything grew very tiny,
Her primness and her sensuality
Locked in a battle of rubber bands
With one clipped petal that she could not free.

After electric shock therapy,
Her memory came back. And with it came
Nothing to remember:
The sea was a toilet for the gulls,
The draperies a possible noose . . .

One night, she woke, and there they stood:
The cruel giants of dependency,
Her mother foaming in front of the piano,
Her father in the kitchen in a rage,
And, looking down, she saw she held
The flower's petals in her hand,
White roses of her guilt, that weed,
—Thorns being her need.

Eva

A sly computer made her clocks all go
At once. She slept inside a spring
Ready to jump up at the hammering
Of six o'clock. "Eva, make the eggs.
Eva, make the coffee, then the beds."
Eva, in a hurry, did. And failed.
Time up. And how she wanted them to go!
Her husband and his body made of hers,
Her children and their bodies made of hers,
And then, alone, another clock would start:
Trapped in a vacuum, she heard her heart
Tick the day away. Two minutes passed.
Two hundred years.

Two zones of feeling wrestled to be free:
To lean upon. Or to be leaned upon.
Scenting danger where it least should be,
She walked out of the house she hated, loved,
And down the street of nothing-to-see
Where everybody else knew the secret. She
Had loved, been loved, could love, was loved,
But like a faded copy of herself,
Growing fainter, she began to disappear.
She turned the corner. There was nothing there.

Miriam

Her long legs stepped across the furniture
And into another world. There stood
A tall girl stepping over furniture
And into another world. Was she
The movie she was watching? Or was she
The girl she watched, watching the movie?
Either way it was "The Miriam Story"
Played by Miriam who was writing the story
Of Miriam playing "The Miriam Story."

The dialogue should have gone like this,
The monologue ("I mean") should have gone like this:

"If you accept me, I will turn away.
If you reject me, I will turn toward you.
I feel so much. Touch me if you can.
And, oh, if I say no, please try again."

Jane

The startling pleasures all broke down,
It was her first arthritic spring.
Inside her furs, her bones, secure,
Suddenly became a source of pain
And froze on a Saturday afternoon
While she was listening to "La Boheme."

Strength had been her weakness, and
Because it was, she got to like
The exhilaration of catastrophes
That prove our lives as stupid as we think,
But pain, more stupid than stupidity,
Is an accident of animals in which, once caught,
The distances are never again the same.

Yet there was another Jane in Jane:
She smelled the inside of a logarithm,
And felt a Gothic arch rise in her chest,
Her clavicle widening to bear the weight
Of the two smooth plumb lines of her breasts,
The blueprints forming an enormous skirt
Around her body. Arch and star and cross
Swung like little lights inside her head,
A church and temple rising from the floor,
Nave and transept and an altar where,
Unbidden, she saw a kind of sacrifice;
The knife was in her hand, the stick, the whip;
She cried at her cruelty and cried to be
Outside of her defenses. And just then,

The windows buckled in, the paintings cracked,
The furniture went walking by itself,
All out of her control. And it was pain
That let her know she was herself again:
She wore a cloak of fire on her skin,
And power, power floated up to her.

Sea Change

At five, nothing but a washrag white,
And one sandpiper pecking at the foam—
A sulphurous saliva drying down.
Drinks are beginning on the porches. Gin
Clear as the light is. On the other side
Of the island, the sunset's foreign stamps,
Great South Bay, and, later, bayside lamps.

At eight, it looks like dirty travertine,
The clouds got up like an old ocarina
Of waxy pink. Then it's not to be seen,
Though something is: the moonlight as a skin
Slicked on each wave, broken on arrival.
A foot falls. Is it onto stone? Or fur?
The whitest sneaker blacks out to a blur.

Night. The passing headlights of a jeep;
The jetties, triple-spaced, the lifeguard stand
Make carbons and go out. And when I turn,
I gather the light's needles in my arms,
The weightlessness of lights, and, falling down
Into a dwarf shadow the moon has drawn,
Or rising up into a giant one,

I waver into wet, stretch out on sheen,
And watch a graduating speck of dawn
Start up the scale from gray to grayish pink,
Turn orange and then red. Soon daylight draws
Two spindles in the distance. Floating in,
Perspective puts a house here, there a dune—
The changing of the gods. Morning. Noon.

On the Library Steps

A bird may build so many nests
Before it dies and think them one
(If it thinks at all), the straw the same,
The twig the same, the fledgling's cry,
And it must feel all woods the same,
Though winds may raise those flimsy wings
And take them south to other woods
Whose leaves and skies are all the same.
And when the similar water falls,
What reaches rock or reigns in clouds
To later fall will fall the same.
And so the hero goes up the steps
Of the library (between two lions
Impossible to tell apart)
To read a treatise on the hero,
And finds ten books about himself—
Their love, his love, the same, the same.

Going to Sleep in the Country

The terraces rise and fall
As the light strides up and rides over
The hill I see from my window.
The spring in the dogwood now,
Enlarging its small preconceptions,
Puts itself away for the night.
The mountains do nothing but sit,
Waiting for something to happen—
Perhaps for the sky to open.

In the distance, a waterfall,
More sound than vision from here,
Is weighing itself again,
A sound you can hardly hear.
The birds of the day disappear,
As if the darkness were final.
The harder it is to see,
The louder the waterfall.

And then the whippoorwill
Begins its tireless, cool,
Calm, and precise lament—
Again and again and again—
Its love replying in kind,
Or blindly sung to itself,
Waiting for something to happen.

In that rain-prickle of song,
The waterfall stays its sound,
Diminishing like a gong
Struck by the weakening hand
Of a walker walking away,
Who is farther away each time,

Until it is finally dumb.
Each star, at a different depth,
Shines down. The moon shines down.
The night comes into its own,
Waiting for nothing to happen.

Painting A Wave

"Painting a wave requires no system,"
The painter said, painting a wave.
"Systems may get you flotsam and jetsam,
Seaweed and so forth. But never a wave."

There was a scroll or fine-lined curve
On the canvas first, and then what looked
Like hair flying or grayish nerves,
Which began to move as the painter worked.

"Painting the sea is a lot of trouble;
It never stops still for a moment, so
I try to make it internal, mental,
As though I stopped it, then let it go."

Something began to pulse and tumble
Out of the brushes, the ink, the chalk;
A long black line commenced to tremble,
Then, like a fishline, started to jerk . . .

With what at the end? "I think I've caught it."
A drop of water hung by a hair.
"If I could only stop it a minute!"
The drop began to race somewhere,

Spreading out in every direction,
A bird of thread, caught in a storm,
Trying to say, "Connection! Action!"
But in the end it was very calm.

Soon there was water under water,
And over the sand a sun . . . a moon?
Who could have seen that wave of water
One night ago? Or a thousand and one?

Who could have seen the lid of water
With its thin mascara of buoys and corks,
With its lined horizon's distant glimmer
Of maybe a skyline like New York's?

Now there will be that morning evening
Tide dyeing the water's pulse,
The wave drying in ink. *The Wave.*
Moving, momentous, motionless.

Movies for the Home

I see the map of summer, lying still,
Its edges under water, blue, fragile.
You cannot hear, of course, from here
The Pacific's portable orchestra—
A kind of shimmery marimba music—
But if you follow all those lines of light,
The nerve-nets of connection, coast to coast,
That screened the days and nights from east to west,
You'll come upon their visions and their sounds:
The dawn's fine print when ink has leaked away,
And a radio turned off still tuned to play
Invisible music. Riding in that car,
I think that where we were is where we are.

The towns the distance fired into being
(By dint of light diagonally drawn
Downward to strike a steeple with a star)
Became fool's gold the closer we came near,
Assembling into lassitudes of palms,
The fresh rot of the wharfs, the hunchbacked hills,
But none of those visions we were driving for.
They drained away, strip cities come and gone,
As if we stayed while we went driving on,
Or they remained where they had never been,
Before us and behind us. They disappeared,
And what at first was flame at last was char.
One wheel turns or another, and there you are.

By supple deviations, twisting on,
The Snake River bent its shapely mail
In moonlight, enlarged and palpable.
The Tetons capped by a display of snow
Refreshed four lakes of summer far below
(Thimblefuls of a barbarian sky);
We dipped our fingers in their sunburnt water
To dribble waterdrops back into blue.
Telegraph wires stitched themselves to trees,
Then dropped away, somewhere in the Rockies.
The pictures pass. We are what we need.
If I remember rightly, we were lost.
We lost the way, being the way we are.

A beautifully painted abstract speed
Lacquered the windshield's cemetery
Of wing and smear so factually there
It seemed the factual was arbitrary
But natural. In those swift ends we saw
The wreckage of ourselves, our wheels in air . . .
Transparent vacancies attack the brain
At one point or another, as if a train
Should smash into a moving mirror of itself
Point-blank high up upon a mountain pass,
And the snow, not even disturbed, give back
Its glacial white indifference to the wreck.
And there, where imagination ends, we are.

Where are we? In a country of lakes?
A Switzerland of Self through which we ski,
Dropping down a lighted scoop of valley
That soon transforms itself into the sea?
(And thus we might arrive at the Impossible:
That place where there is nothing left to see.)
Now we are standing on a wooden pier
Watching the Pacific stun itself on rocks;
If the camera stopped, if you could stare
Out far enough, the Orient, over there,
Might have the excitement of intense boredom.
Our house in Berkeley? You turn the corner there,
Go left and down the hill, and there you are.

Alongside water all the afternoon,
The sea so far below we could not fall,
What threatened ending rose from its abyss
To rattle in the tin can of the car?
Was it the blue that flaked away to cloud,
The green that flew away on either side,
The white-lined serpent of the road ahead,
Intense as distance in its silences,
That colored what we thought until we thought:
The color of the distance is the color bled
Out of the time it takes to get us there?
The pictures pass. We are the way we were.
Being here and there is what we are.

By going forward we were coming back.
When the film rewinds, you'll see what I mean,
In the woods, that lipsticked drinking cup,
Stuck in the drying margins of the stream,
Turns up again in the desert coming up
Quite soon in malignant iodine and green.
Now we are looking at an estuary
Whose waters gently poach an evening star
Whose spidery edges are collapsing down
As far as the eye can see, but just so far.
I wonder if you can go as far as far
And still not see things as they really are,
Only as they were, if that is where you are.

The Snow Weed

Last summer's weed sprang from my window box,
A perseverant marvel; I let it hatch
Into a lyre-branch of small sunflowers
That never quite turned gold. Today, for hours
It snowed, and when it stopped, the sun came out,
Ghostly, at first, like a dim parachute,
Then its summer self, hotheaded, prodigal,
Blazing at the cold. The weed stood tall,
Thrust up from a snowbank, with more snow to come,
A fan-shaped skeleton, or wide whisk broom,
A peacock tail but colorless. All form,
Adaptable to cold as it was to warm,
It swayed upon its root, remaining firm,
And bore a second blossoming of storm.

September Elegy

The dead undo our sleep so they can rest.
Their August vanishes: the beachy dreams
Of sea grass, naked limbs, the stuttering wave . . .
Yet contra-indicated bodies move
On space . . . the summer sprays, the water birds
Depart, but some things never disappear,

The faces of the dead: one drowned, one hurled,
Drunk, through a subway window to be smashed
Against an iron post, one burned to ash
In Key West, Florida, and one whose heart,
Clogged up, destroyed the finest wit of all.
The world of pain is one great hospital.

Guilt feeds on the inconsequential. Leaves
Took light upon themselves in California when
The eucalyptus shed their strange, dry smell
Of sweat and alcohol on a long drive back
Of Grizzly Peak above the Berkeley Hills,
Whose houses fling themselves into the bay,

Perspective racing down a staircase. When
The sun deposed itself, the stars were low,
So low we had to walk around them. In
A house in Millbrook, watercress at stream,
Black Angus in the distance, the shaved lime-green
Of hills some miles away, I thought where are

Those companies that once surrounded me?
They troop into my room tonight, my heart-
Beat numb among the thunders of their sea;
Revived against all probability,
A wave reversed, a turning leaf turned green,
They rise up from the ground to smother me.

The leaves that fall. Each calendar is full
   Of them, whose turnings burn away in time.
Aesthetic distance primes the beautiful,
   In this case doubly, for dead leaves renew
Themselves, but what the dead can never do,
   They do in dreams, who break the night into

Three landscapes—scrims that any theatre can
   Re-reconstruct. Though places have no will,
Refocused in the night, they soon compel
   The watcher to be witness of a scene
Behind the scenes, as if two curtains fell
   On each side of another, and when each rose,

One by one, revealed a triple world:
   The seen, the recollected, and the scene
To come, all lit at once, whose figures stain
   Each meaning with another meaning, whose
Cruelties outdo past cruelties,
   The lightning of their blood now branched in mine.

Into the camera where two hairs cross
   To center them, their frosty breaths arrive,
And then their faces, bodies, and their cold
   Voices saying, "You are still alive!"
And, in the babble of their monologues,
   The old and deadly arguments begin.

Assuage them, talk. They are relentless. They
   Remember everything. What I deny
They soon prove true. They probe below the will
   To tear identity to shreds. And still
They are not satisfied. In rooms that spring
   Up on the way, they judge, condemn, and kill.

Trees turn the slender dowels of their arms.
    At last, the sea drowns summer in a wave.
See how the little wooden houses storm
    The dune edge, how slowly coming down
Five leaves are spelling what the autumn is.
    There is an end, even of houses.

I turn away from those black speakers. More
    Leaves fall, and, falling, comment on the time
And Time—the thin clock faces winding down
    In spinning parachutes suggest that autumn
When I will rend the watches of the night
    In someone else's sleep—someone who will

Fall also. The sleep that takes it all!
    The slowly rusting graduates of spring,
Schooled in one history to which they cling,
    Divest themselves of knowledge, and begin
To flake away, to file into the ground.
    After the dazzlement, the colors die;

From undressed hills, old skeletons arise;
    The sky leaks through them, the high blue days
Of absolute lucidity have flown
    Onto a sea glazed colder. Ocean sound
Recedes. It is noon now. The voices stay
    Asleep, their bodies hidden, their spirits numb.

New forms of light are lifting up the air,
    The narrow surfboard of the thigh's ashore,
And summer's over. A beacon for the pulse,
    One cracked star freezes in the thinnest ice,
And, mapped toward its ending, the last late leaf
    Settles on my upturned, aging hand.

History

It takes more lies than anyone can tell,
Babbling lies a lifetime, to tell the lies
History has told, the mythic apple
A rotted fruit from Eve to William Tell—
Those two arch overtures. Great Hannibal,
Who put the Roman armies in his till,
Drank poison from a ring. Ecclesiastical
Charlemagne, inspired by an angel,
Thought his world was permanent. It was, until . . .

Long after the Armada turned to Pearl,
Middle-class Victoria in night shift woke
To save the Empire, that little girl.
And there were days when Cleopatra, ill,
Said, "Dump diplomacy into the Nile.
Caesar I'm sick of, and Mark you well,
I do not think the sea swell will prevail
For me to tag along beside his sail."
So saying with her asp she gasped farewell.

Farewell, Napoleon, enisled at last,
Who plunged all Europe into his blood bath,
A half-pint Corsican, engorged by war.
Thus, too, did General Grant assay the South.
Ashes, he thought, it comes to in the end.
And Hadrian, the biggest swell of all,
Whose villa all for love now lies in ruins,
No longer cares where Asia's borders are.
"Antinous," he said, "Fare well, Farewell."

Said one, entrenched, "This war is one long sell.
What world is this in which I live to kill?
Is that sound Roland's horn at Roncesvalles
I hear . . . ?" They stopped the question with a shell.
A Chinese emperor reared back in pain
To see his blood not jade upon the snow.
Meanwhile, in Spain, the Inquisition reigned,
And carnage was general in Mexico.

So stood they in the marsh or tramped the sea,
With salt-burned eyes or flesh that cracked in oil;
Bodies before the gate jerked up and fell;
In No Man's Land, the corpses lay pell mell.
"Power is what I wanted till I got it,"
One cried, "My kingdom is in bloody rout!"
"The God is here," slim Montezuma said;
Into Tenochtitlan he led Cortez,
Whose world was permanent. Until it was.

The Pruned Tree

As a torn paper might seal up its side,
Or a streak of water stitch itself to silk
And disappear, my wound has been my healing,
And I am made more beautiful by losses.
See the flat water in the distance nodding
Approval, the light that fell in love with statues,
Seeing me alive, turn its motion toward me.
Shorn, I rejoice in what was taken from me.

What can the moonlight do with my new shape
But trace and retrace its miracle of order?
I stand, waiting for the strange reaction
Of insects who knew me in my larger self,
Unkempt, in a naturalness I did not love.
Even the dog's voice rings with a new echo,
And all the little leaves I shed are singing,
Singing to the moon of shapely newness.

Somewhere what I lost I hope is springing
To life again. The roofs, astonished by me,
Are taking new bearings in the night, the owl
Is crying for a further wisdom, the lilac
Putting forth its strongest scent to find me.
Butterflies, like sails in grooves, are winging
Out of the water to wash me, wash me.
Now, I am stirring like a seed in China.

Finding Them Lost

Thinking of words that would save him, slanting
Off in the air, some cracked, some bent;
Finding them lost, he started saying
Some other words he never meant.

The green went back and forth in waves
As if his heart pumped out the lawn
In blood, not grass. A bench sailed down,
Becoming the bench he sat upon,

Staring out at the crazy garden,
With its women washed out to milky shades,
Or pressed through the trees' accordion,
While the past jerked past in lantern slides,

Badly lit, of images unbidden,
Faces, arms, and forgotten eyes
That, peeping through the leaves, half hidden,
Turned on and off like fireflies.

Fire and flies. *That* was it,
He thought, as the nurse bloomed, coming, coming
Straight through a tree to hold his hand.
Holding hers, he felt blood drumming

Through the twined bones of where they met.
It was three months the stubborn grass
Wouldn't rise up to meet his foot,
Or, rising up, caught him unawares.

Sleep, it was sleep, that found him napping
When the delicious dew of sweat
Brought forth the baby he'd been hiding
Wrapped in his skin, maybe his heart.

And what the mirror gave back was him
Finally, tired and very old.
"My life, begin . . ." But it didn't, wouldn't,
Though grass was grass and no bench sailed

Down to a garden to support him
And no one walked through a tree to hold
His hand. But a green lawn pulses in him.
Home, he still dreams of going home.

From Second Nature *(1968)*

Sands

1

Dry. The wind is parched by the wind.
The stars are machines whose needlepoints
Stab through the throat. Crazed by thirst,
That dog must be killed. Don't cry. Please don't.
It's a waste of water. Yes, I know
The sand is hotter than you can stand,
But, surely, since we have come this far. . . .

2

You'd be surprised
How the body endures
Suffering. What else can it do?
Oh, the mind. That's different. Close your eyes,
And just keep going. Did I ever tell
You stories of Cortez, Ghenghis Khan,
And Hannibal—quite ordinary men?
If we stop now, it will be harder in
The morning. Think of the risk of sun.

3

I'm sorry I said that. Concentrate
On images and dreams, on wanted things
Like streams, springs, and rivulets. . . .
It makes it worse? Think of nothing, then,
But the blood that flows from head to foot
And back, of the brain's banked oxygen,
Of how footfall must follow tread,
If you will it to. You can stand the pain.
Do it for my sake. I ask again.

4

I think the path has become obscure.
The map's inaccurate. I cannot read
The compass because the flashlight's failed,
And we're out of matches. Besides, I think
It was off last time. It's hard to be sure.
Have faith in me. Have faith in me.
Think of all those who have gone before.

5

There must be a country somewhere right now
Of rain, of snow, of golden wind
Where, in the rushes, all that play
Of watery hazards takes the mind.
And that must be the country of joy,
That country that we will never find.
Or perhaps we will. Now we must rest,
Before the sand makes us blind.

6

Only so many miles to go,
And ages in which to do it. So
I like to think. The dog is dead.
I swear
There should be water soon.
We must wait. And wait. The sun's too high.
We'll begin again at the end of day.

7
My darling,
Not to have made it is
To kill, and kill,
And be killed again.
Now, only your body lies
In my bodiless arms,
So dead, so still,

And there is the oasis, up ahead.

The Building

Removed by half a city, not the world,
I see the building you are working in.
It is a winter day. The branches clash
On the few trees that mark the avenue.
If I could go to where I wanted to,
How would I find you? As you were before?
Or are you like the person I've become,
Far into the dark, and far from home?

This winter day was not so dark before
That light was lost that only you could know.
When I go home, and then the dark comes home,
The branches clash along the avenue.
If you could go, I think I'd want you to,
Somewhere the building you'd be working in
Would be a world away, and far from home.
I'm far into the dark when far from you,

And this is something only you could know:
I'm not the person that I was before
You went into the dark. In finding you,
I used to go just where I wanted to.
On the few trees that mark the avenue
The branches clash. It is a winter day.
I see the building you are working in
Removed by half a city, and the world.

Piano Practice

For Frances Dillon Haywood

1

Such splendid icecaps and hard rills, such weights
And counter-weights, I think I scale the heights
When pentatonic Chinese crewmen start
Up in a cold sweat from the bottom of the keyboard
Only to arrive at some snow-stormed valley
To dissolve in steam-holes and vanish out of sight.

2

The left hand's library is dull, the books
All read, though sometimes, going under velvet,
An old upholsterer will spit out tacks,
Turn them into sparks and smartly hurl them
Up and down the loudest bowling alley—
His pressure of effects can last all night.

3

Two bird notes endlessly repeat themselves.
Or are they fish scales—iridescent, hard?
Mica into marble back to mica?
No images in trills. They're formal. Take
Your foot off the pedal. You're in a wood
Near the sea. And every tree and wave is fake.

4

An underwater haircut by Debussy?
Oh, that's too easy. Astringent lotions
Let the swimmer down by easy stages
Down among the flashy soda fountains
Down to the bottom where the light bulbs waver
Down where all the mirrors eat their hearts out.

5
Grammar becoming poetry is what
You're after—say, a rational derangement
Requiring that you forget technique
And concentrate on what is harder like
A fireplace that burns pine needles only,
Before which spills the gore of Persian rugs.

6
A vial of antiseptic meant for Schubert,
One modest, flat meticulous translation
Of Chopin's lightning undercurrent Spanish—
These are the mere necessities of travel.
Someone you must meet is Dr. Czerny.
Then, through him, Domenico Scarlatti.

7
Seizures are occurring. Despite snow-lightning,
The black keys are bent on mountain climbing—
All of it against a doctor's warning.
Soon they're descending like the black dots of
A wirephoto in transmission. An
Erotic black wing hovers up above.

8
Bach is more like opening an ember
And digging hard into the heart of fire.
The heart of fire is another fire.
When it comes to Mozart, just say nothing.
Think of it as milk, and drink it slowly.
Slowly you will taste the cream of angels.

9

This black and white's deceptive. Underneath
The spectrum rages. Did you ever see
The calmest waters quickly come to life
Because a minnow's tinfoil flash in sun
Had rent them suddenly? It came. And went.
We take two thousand takes before we print.

10

Don't try to catch that lion by Rousseau.
Before you wake, he'll eat you up. If you
Should meet the sleeping gypsy, let her sleep.
Tomorrow they'll be gone without a trace,
Half fact and half enigma. Now your hands
Are on the mysteries of the commonplace.

The Bay Stone

The bay's translucency—a thin shellac
Of armor taken off—has taken back
Each chisel stroke of tide, each gallery
The pigments of the world drilled into rock.
This stone is not the stone it used to be.

One membrane still revives it: moisture's touch
Can brush the nerves of fern and fissure back:
Imbedded stress of tiny trees of rust,
Rosettes, and the false sunsets water makes
Before dry air unpaints the stone again.

Because you chose it, your stone is the one
That drops through time to bring all others back
To where anonymously still they drown,
Reflecting vacantly that vacant day,
The day before the bay turned into stone.

Great Spaces

I would worship if I could
Man, woman, child, or dog,
Strip the desert from my back,
Spill an ocean from each eye,
And like those saints who trust to luck

Sit for years under a tree.
I live now in a dirty city
That prowls the sky and is my shade;
Only a low, uneasy light
Gathers there, a light low-keyed

Amid great spaces and great times.
They soon grow smaller. I forget
What months and years once swam through me
As I walked into their great rooms,
Forgotten rooms, forgotten scenes,

And out in space a statue stands
That will not gloss its meaning. Near
Its pedestal, and on its hands
And knees, a figure, wild, unshorn,
Lifts its head to speak. It says,

"Nothing is unwilling to be born."

The Meeting

It never occurred to me, never,
That you were attached to your universe,
Standing on a corner, waiting for a bus,
While the thought-trees grew above your head
And a meadow stretched its rambling sward
All the way up Fifth Avenue.
I was thinking of myself thinking of water,
Of how, each day I went about my job,
I missed one break in the Atlantic Ocean,
Of how I might have been here or there,
Fishing off the coast of Mexico,
Turning the sailboat round the bay,
Or, my chin resting on the concrete edge
Of a swimming pool, I could survey a hill,
The cows' soft blotches stranded in the grass.
Maybe it was that, that last green thing,
That led me into your deepening meadow,
That made me turn among the giant stones
To look one minute into your mind,
To see you running across a field,
The flowers springing up where you had touched.
It was there, I think, we finally met.

Front Street

1

The moon's little skullcap,
Dry divinity,
Has brought all color
Into question:
What is your skin now—
Lime or gray?
It has a kind of phosphorescent shine.
Fluorescent? Is that what I mean?
There are no words to describe it.

2

That greasy tug
Might be a spy,
That flashing lens
A trained binocular.
A death rattle has obsessed the tree
And a strangling sound the harbor water,
Which keeps saying, "Don't count on me!"—
As if we were such fools
To count on it ever!

3

I'm sorry the sick palms look so rundown,
That Front Street, which used to be so gay,
Seems like the street of a plague-ridden town—
Empty, apprehensive, dirty.
Do not go down the steps into the boat.
A storm is coming.
Can't you hear the wind?
Do you think I enjoy being arbitrary?
Do what I say.
Or else we'd better say goodbye right now.

4

Why did I bring you to Front Street? Because
The boats are here,
In case we have to make a quick get-away.
All right. Call it irrational fear.
The Jews in Germany, one year before
They saw the handwriting on the wall,
Would have thought you mad
If you'd told them where
They'd all end up. Think of Oedipus
A second before the blind seer opened his mouth.
No. We're not going back.
We're going some place. Anywhere.
Somewhere we can be, temporarily, safe.

5

You think nature's a left-handed compliment?
A French one's more like it;
I could have told you, twenty years ago,
It's a dirty dig. Think of a time,
Five years, or one,
When people weren't at each other's throats.
Everywhere there are miles of files
With our names typed in them, yours and mine.
The point is to be invisible
Or blinding, nothing in between—
Famous or anonymous . . .
But it's much too late for people like us.

6
O.k. O.k. We'll go back to the house.
A false alarm?
What a child you are!
Remember when we get back into town,
And the sun's shining, oh, so bright,
And everything seems so right, so fine,
So permanent,
Front Street will be waiting at our backs.

Particular Beauties

Whether it was a particular beauty
Stirred the tearfall from the eyelid's rim,
Rinsing the world once more with self,
Was it not there the general peered,
Thousand-eyed, down from the peak
In the last of all imaginary sunsets?
The light divided in half, the half
Divided again in half, the way
Zeno's paradox makes nothing move
Because an infinity of points between
Target and arrow, though never seen,
Exists. And there is snow in a capsule,
A solid floor of individual
Flakes that, shaken, settle in a field—
Parachutists growing where the grass,
One moment before, was only natural.
I am speaking now of the diminishment
Or enhancement of enchanted objects,
Of how they turn into nothingness
Or burnish the imagination:
A fire at the bottom of the sea,
For instance, or a mind in space
Thinking its way into science fiction,
Or, inside the skull, a little world
Clinging, about to be thrown away—
Miraculous lint under a bell.

At the Algonquin

He sat at the Algonquin, smoking a cigar.
A coffin of a clock bonged out the time.
She was ten minutes late. But in that time,
He puffed the blue eternity of his cigar.

Did she love him still? His youth was gone.
Humiliation's toad, with its blank stares
Squatted on his conscience. When they went upstairs,
Some version of them both would soon be gone.

Before that, though, drinks, dinner, and a play—
The whole demanding, dull expense account
You paid these days for things of no account.
Whatever love may be, it's not child's play.

Slowly she walked toward him. God, we are
Unnatural animals! The scent of roses
Filled the room above the carpet's roses,
And, getting up, he said, "Ah, *there* you are!"

The Persistence of Song

Although it is not yet evening,
The secretaries have changed their frocks
As if it were time for dancing,
And locked up in the scholars' books
There is a kind of rejoicing,
There is a kind of singing
That even the dark stone canyon makes
As though all fountains were going
At once, and the color flowed from bricks
In one wild, lit upsurging.

What is the weather doing?
And who arrived on a scallop shell
With the smell of the sea this morning?
—Creating a small upheaval
High above the scaffolding
By saying, "All will be well.
There is a kind of rejoicing."

Is there a kind of rejoicing
In saying, "All will be well?"
High above the scaffolding,
Creating a small upheaval,
The smell of the sea this morning
Arrived on a scallop shell.
What was the weather doing

In one wild, lit upsurging?
At once, the color flowed from bricks
As though all fountains were going,
And even the dark stone canyon makes
Here a kind of singing,
And there a kind of rejoicing,
And locked up in the scholars' books
There is a time for dancing
When the secretaries have changed their frocks,
And though it is not yet evening,

There is the persistence of song.

Beach Glass

Mr. Calava rises at five
A.M., the first on the beach, but not
Because he's crazy about the sea.
He's crazy about beach glass. He has
Two thousand pieces
At the latest count.
An industry of idleness,
He's a connoisseur of broken glass.

Sucked candy bits as hard as lava,
The shards are no longer sharp and come
In every shape and every color—
The commonest are white and brown:
Harder to find are blue and green;
Amber is rare; yellow rarer;
And red the rarest of all. The sea's

A glass-blower who blasts to bits
Coca-Cola and Waterford,
Venetian as well as Baccarat,
And has carefully combed its five-and-ten
For anything made of glass. It isn't
Fussy. It knows that everything
Will be pared down in the end:
Milk of magnesia bottles honed
To sky-blue icy filaments,
And smoky cordial bottles from
Brazil—sunglasses of an eclipse.

Mr. Calava's kaleidoscopes
Are kept in apothecary jars,
As if the sea were a pharmacy
Of lozenges and doled them out
Without a prescription, especially
For Mr. Calava, who firmly believes
The best things in life are free.

But what the sea has relinquished it
Has relinquished only in part. You know
How childish it is in its irony.
The jig-saw puzzle is here. But then
Its missing pieces are still in the sea.
Not all the king's horses and all the king's men
Could ever put it together again,
Though—chip by chip
And bit by bit—

Rouault could make a King of it.

The Vase

Before the summer flowers fell,
I set the vase of autumn out,
And in that spare receptacle
Pure form alone exists without

The feasibility of bloom
And takes the sky into its depth,
A skylight in a living room
Whose walls are slowly papered with

Dead leaves on dead, until those walls—
The curved sides of the vase—rise up,
Revealing endless vestibules,
Those alleys where each shadowgraph

Is still the shadow of a vase
No longer there. I wake to no
Paint boxes stacked against the skies
To hear the rainpipe drip of snow.

Arsenic

They will be telling you soon who you are,
The importunate, slovenly younger thinkers—
But only because they are young. From afar,
You may hear certain familiar voices,
Romantic but growing increasingly dim,
Express themselves in some thirty sounds
Out of a possible twenty thousand;
The terraces will be swinging in place
With their few discordant violins, the lamps
Hissing with gas, the smell of an old
Shoebox suddenly tainting the wharf—
Or could the sky's incredible liquor
Be responsible for the odor of
A set of ancient mah-jongg tiles
You found in your mother's closet once?
What are they doing here on the coast?
They are lusterless now from disuse and the sun.

> *"I have taken a sufficient dose and still*
> *Feel nothing, a slight burning sensation*
> *But no smell of garlic, the telltale sign.*
> *Strange. And several seconds have passed.*
> *No pain. But for those who follow, I note*
> *That the phone will appear farther away . . ."*

Now they will tell you your favorite words,
Symbols gone sickly with use—such as
Gull blue ocean house—
Are no longer possible. And they're right.
You *have* been a bit of a fool. You have
Been feeling your way
When you should have gone straight
To the heart of the matter. Which is what?
To have looked humiliation full
In the face instead of walking around
It, like a dog chained to a pole . . .

For instance, a letter arrived this week,
Saying
            "You're not expressing yourself.
              It's hard to know who you are."
These facts
Are relevant:
I have never killed.
I have loved three times—
Possibly four—
I have two suits
I will never wear.
The mornings are bad,
But by evening I'm
Myself again.

Do you know me now, Miss Mandarin?
You of the scented, mauve-lined page
Who tell me that you were once a nun

But now, when a sailor stalks the streets,
You feel the old magic welling up,
The thing most of all you're afraid to lose?
Don't tell me *you're* the one who wrote
Three hundred times on a warehouse wall
"Don't knock love!" If so, I shake
Your hand still blue from chalk. . . .

3 THE THIRD LETTER

But there it is. One word
Used up already. Blue.
And here's another, thinly disguised:

Meanwhile the sea, a hundred yards away,
Already bored with its literary career,
Is beating itself up, again, again,
And, sick of the moon's attentions every night,
Is carving a sandbar farther out
Behind which it hopes to draw its skirts
And thus avoid the shore's vulgar display.
It's deluded, of course. It isn't very bright.
But it's beautiful. Which, around here, is right.

Now I am going back to the house
For a drink. From the upper porch, I see
A gull go by on the steadiest wings
You ever saw. If a scavenger's
That gorgeous, what will they say of me?
There's something to be said for everything.
For garbage, for instance, in this case.

"I've been meaning to write much sooner but
Something has kept me from saying just
What I wanted to . . . Are you well? Does J.
Still wake each night and need comforting?
I think, perhaps, that the lack of love,
Yes, love . . . I feel you no longer
Love, sincerely, with a thousand thoughts . . ."

Starlight, dear walk, when this view is
Nothing but emptied space and snow,
When no foot breaks its silences,
What faces, guests will then arrive
Frantic with their reasons to live?

Another Life

There might be the quibble of birds and the swag
Of a river and a distantly belled
Altar of animals, softly spoken;
Certainly cattail, sumac, and fern
Would rise from the marshes nearby, revealed
In forms too perfect to envy trees—
Not trying for larger and larger keepsakes.

Cryptic and subtle green, hedgerows
Hiding mysterious deer, the start
Of a rabbit, as if towers and clouds
Had suddenly shadowed an open field—
These would be the events of the day,
Life having narrowed down to please
Natural hungers and thirsts, the grass
Thick at our feet, and, above our heads,
The stars, their firework anemones.

What shall I say of the house? Or you?
Only industrious ghosts would know
How lazily cropping up the view
Would make the impossible possible;
Nothing but weekdays would blankly graze
On time's oblivious pastures, free
At last of motive and thought, and we,
Becoming ourselves so naturally,
Would never say, looking up at the sky,
Another life is shining in the sky.

The Maid's Story

Between her leaving Cobh
And putting the kettle on
Each morning on the stove,
Twenty springs had gone.

A slow flutter of nerves
Told her the slow truth:
There was to be no love
In heaven or on earth.

She never could put the losses
In words, never could say—
When they asked, "What's the matter?"—
What was the matter. They

Were patient and impatient
Like the city she stared at.
She was lint in the clothes closet.
She was dust under the rug.

She stayed that way for years,
In between loss and loss;
Each night, she dreamed of a house
That was hers. It never was.

Then less and less mattered,
Each day was just each day.
Finally nothing mattered,
She opened her mouth to say.

Going Dutch

1

Two gloves, a lipstick, and a corduroy
Bag, a saucer filling up with butts. . . .
A check will soon be coming to their joy,
That joy they nourish on their separate cots.
They halve the bill and take a flying walk
Up Fifth. A rip of blue. And then it's dark.

A bar. The old songs. Who remembers now
That dated country of a five o'clock
Piano tinkling out its moving, shallow
Tune that gives the heart its little knock?
The sentimental is so trivial,
One gin erases it or brings it back.

They're home now. Separately. She sprays her hair,
Puts down her cigarette, afraid of fire,
While he takes down a book he's read before;
Starting it, he starts to think of her—
The dream: Her figure floating up the stair,
His floating down, not going anywhere.

2

"'Judas.' 'Three.' Those words are in my head,"
She said, and drew a circle in the ash—
Cigarette ash in which a sybil read
On the tabletop with all its dirty wash.
How many years had passed between the two?
Fifteen? Twenty? Nothing seemed to change:
Her flint of beauty staggered on one shoe,
His crooked insight wandered out of range.
"But am I menaced? And by whom?" he asked.

The sybil spoke in wonders and in dreads:
"Beware the envious. Stay quiet. Work.
In six months, maybe you'll be safe." The reds
And whites of a checkered cloth were shaken free;
A piece of old French bread, a glass of wine
Were put back on the table. Close to three,
They sat as if their money were their time.

3
Strange, the validity of the past,
As if the sound of distant traffic
Slowly floated up to consciousness,
A small jazz combo at the bottom of the ocean
Disturbed by somebody's auxiliary motor,
Or the thunder of the sea as the waves pass.

Still Pond, No More Moving

I

They have taken the maps and spread them out
And parted from each other,
Have slipped the rivers into their veins
And pocketed the sandy beaches,
Have gone walking through slow trains
Across where the Mississippi bends,
Have gone in even slower freighters
Down the irregular coastlines—
The inlet's curve, the island's nest
Lure them along a dotted line
Back or forward, forward or back,
And some have settled at an address.

Above them all the same sky
Shapes the mountain or meets the shore,
And some—now undecided why
They chose one or the other—stare
Out of a crooked window from
A ramshackle cabin on a dune
At the slow rollers coming in,
The sheets hung out on a clothesline,
While the children's disparate cries
Rise up from the hard shore,
And someone is looking up
Wishing that he were where
The pines soar to the mountaintop
Or stop at the snowline.

2

Is it water they want, water,
The sea changingly in,
Or, cool to the tilted diver
Ringed round by quarry walls,
The stills of deep water
That make him weightless, blind,
As he soars back to the beginning,
That spring without a mind?
Or the highest mountain places
Where the sudden shaded lake
Refreshes the eye because
No two lakes are alike?

And sometimes by its absence—
Or by its opposite—
Water is strangely felt:
In New Mexico, appearance
Conceived as existence springs
Forward into the distance
In vanishing parallels
Of skylines of lighted cliffs
That race up to the hills;
The desert, its own mirage,
Breaks in wave on wave
Between the bloodied mountains
At the running out of day,
And when the sun says it is
Life and death at once,
There, in the few trees,
Water stands up to dance.

3

And some are far out at sea.
The horizon is growing dark.
Someone is taking a walk
On the deck of a dipping hull—
Or the deck awash in a storm—
Barely holding on—
While some at the ship's bar
Sit while an arm extends
Their gin and their caviar,
And find with the first sip
The seepage of doubt begin:
Oh, what did I come for?
What am I doing here?
Supposing the lights went off
And we stopped right where we are?

4

Who is painting the barn door?
Who is painting the painter there,
Summer after summer,
The summer plucked from the year?
But there is that one summer
When old age, like a stick
Thrown for a retriever
Who does not bring it back,
Keeps drifting farther out
Till it's no longer seen—
One mountainside slides down,
One city street slams shut,
A piece of the sea is gone.

Is it Hythe or Rockaway?
Or the Puerto Rican waves
That roll in in the same way?
Or Rosarita Beach
Where the sulphur of the sand
Is marked by the horse's hoof,
And the Moorish hotel stands,
A white elephant, aloof,
Where once the gamblers jammed
The tables, and now one goes
Into almost empty rooms
And the four guitarists come
To the table to serenade?

5

I know some landscapes where
Intensity comes late,
And, deepening in light,
Brings such an inner peace
That floating by in the gold
The world is half dissolved
And the last birds cry farewell
To the day and the shadows seem
To lean on the trees in the wood.

And others where morning comes
Spun out on a crystal web,
And innocence is abroad
And drinks in the new-made world,
And nothing appears to be
Violent or amiss,
And silence would be a tree,
Except that the wind is.

6

Someone is bitterly thinking
The innermost's not said:
Where is the great theme?
Whoever saw the world
At once and saw it whole?
In New England now,
Here where the water is,
Here where the red barn
Is an advocate of hills,
Time rigs up famous shapes,
The white whales, the white ships,
Yet in summer's lapse
The drunken sea bards come
To lounge on all its Capes.

The Dune Wig

Ice had hollowed out the dunes, dead trees
Thrust roots into the air along that coast
Where all was lost for trees, where all was lost
For you and me; the desolation there
Brought winter into heat: the glacial frost
The rocks made visible, the dune's dry wigs—
The still-felt analogues of old affairs.
The bay weed's thick Sargasso webbed us in
So that each footstep, taking time, made time
A slower crepitation at the rim.

Bay gravel shook inside a tambourine.
I watched you walking out to see the dead
Horseshoe crab, its limp and twisted meat
Hanging from its shell, a floating mine.
Something like a sunburst rocked my head,
Burning in to touch me—as you had.
Since love is of the body, since your hand
Is still imprinted on my skin, I bear
The mark of Scandinavian countries
That were the gold dune-grasses of your hair.

Drinks with X

"Yes, Paris is lovely from a balcony,"
The woman says. The woman in black.
I look down at the Rue de Wolfe. There are
Several imposing hotels and one
Café where a hunchbacked man writes notes.
The waitress is fanning away the flies.
It's August. Most of the French are away.
A few people walk up and down the streets.

She says, "I have my exotic birds,
My pianos tinkling with absence, cakes
Yet to be eaten by queens, blue seas
Hung up in sunny courtyards to dry,
And slides made of ice with love details
Still thought to be pornographic by
The vulgar—those who have never loved.
I, who have nibbled at everything,

Develop the negatives of the heart
At a glance. The heart, oh, the heart," she cries.
"Naturally, cruelty comes into it
Since we are all egotistical,
But let me assure you again I will
Be waiting patiently at the end
When, waking from summer's sluggish dream,
You crash into snow. Just think of me

As old disappointment's youngest child,
Modest but sly, with ten thousand veils
To screen the Soul from Reality—
The thing is to say goodbye to the past,
Then cultivate the remains. Who's *here*?
Is always the question one should ask.
Too many tears have been shed in vain,
And for what? Half-loaves of love or fame. . . .

When I think of the possibilities!
Get out a map or walk five blocks
Away from your usual daylight haunts.
(Only a fool would revise the night!)
Civilization and nature both
Can offer such startling illusory gifts:
The sunset having its heart attack,
The telephone wires' encephalogram.

And now, I'm afraid we must part. Goodbye.
Thank you so much for the splendid view,
Which combines the banal and spectacular.
I would have preferred so much more to be
At home, engrossed in a mystery—
And aren't we *all* engrossed in one?—
Or worse, smoking myself to death,
Ha ha, in front of my tiny TV. . . .

One last word. I'd avoid the beach
If I were you, and not just because
We're not as young as we used to be.
How true it is that the old clichés
Say the most! How's that? My tiny TV?
Oh, yes, of course we have them here.
And *there*, too. But I must. . . . Bonjour.
And don't forget: I'll be seeing you."

The Wars

How can I tell you of the terrible cries
Never sounded, of the nerves that fail,
Not in jungle warfare or a southern jail,
But in some botched affair where two people sit
Quite calmly under a blood-red lamp
In a Chinese restaurant, a ludicrous swamp
Of affection, fear drowning in the amber
Tea when no word comes to mind
To stand for the blood already spilled,
For rejection, denial, for all those years
Of damage done in the polite wars?

And what do I know of the terrible cries
That are really sounded on the real hill
Where the soldiers sweat in the Asian night
And the Asians sweat where the soldiers flail
The murderous grass, and the peasants reel
Back in a rain of gasoline,
And the shells come home and the bombs come down
Quite calmly under a blood-red moon
Not far from China, and the young are killed,
Mere numerals in the casualties
Of this year's war, and the war of years?

He stands with a knife in the Daily News.
They are snaking their way into the hills.
She is walking up Broadway to hurt again.
They are fleeing under a hail of shells.
He is taking her neck into his hands.
A human seed squats in the dark.
She is scalding the baby in the bath.
He feels the bullet enter his skin.
She spits in the face of the riot squad.
They are sitting down, they are opening wounds.

The Love Songs of Horatio Alger, Jr.

About to fall in love
With someone I won't remember
A decade from now, I tie
The knot in my best bowtie
And stumble down twenty stairs
And cross ten streets of rain,
And then it all starts again . . .

You take this old address:
Somebody lived here once.
I couldn't even guess
The name, the face, but once

I raced up twenty stairs
And nobody was in,
And I walked slowly down.

Is it the rain, the rain
That makes me feel again
What I thought I couldn't feel?
The sound of the rainfall,
Hardly a sound at all.

2

Walking the wet macadam for
The alterations of the night,
I dream the dream of in between:
The sad and indecisive street
Where crippled children skate at five,
Where their wax crutches melt in light.

I see the madman's eyes insist
On taking children home to bed
To weave of them his hair and skin,
His nest, his love, his window scene,
Until the crow at the violet hour
Comes with black songs in his throat
To sing of coincidence and murder.

3

I cherish most the libidinous moment
When, striving done, with a sensual comment,
I ransom back my golden will.
The city of stars within my skull
Stops circling. When its sky is still,
That mouth I kissed, those eyes that teared
Lie dead, and I'm King Lear out-Leared,
For though my storm was all light verse,
Its lines still shook my universe.

Concrete ribbons shine in the dark
Among the stilted lakes and trees
Slick with reflected light, the fake
Cuts, montages, and bad re-takes
Of rainy Saturday movie scenes.
My heart that once leaked gold I now
Hold back, my mistresses disappear
Into the quicksand of the years,
But I shall join them when I shed
These dollar signs that are my eyes,
This ticker tape that is my brain,
When, with my wallet full, I fall
Into the biggest deal of all.

A Dead Leaf

Today, the first dead leaf in the hall
Is surprised, taking on its second nature,
To find that trees are forms of furniture;
The earliest message to arrive from winter,
It's too far gone, indoors or out,
To eat the sun or drink the water,
And I, I am more desperate than ever,
Reading the memoirs that Madame Blank
Keeps sending on in thick installments.
Twelve publishers have firmly declined. . .
(Thank God! For I am thinly disguised
As yet another form of furniture:
My name is Harrod—a character
Who at one point rather stupidly remarks,
"Only a Fool could love King Lear.")
Madame would hate these opening lines;
She is against both cadence and meter.

Armories, windows,
Days and weeks
Of peering out, then drawing back—
Is there enough artillery
To blast the gossips of this block?
Paranoia is a borderline
Without a country on either side.
That fortress of brownstones across the way
Is money talking
With nothing to say.

Rectitude and impropriety!
I have given them both up,
And settled for a sleazy mysticism,
Befuddled rain and poisoned mist;
Sometimes I'm so depressed I think
It's *life* that's the anesthetist.
But then I wake quite sane, as if
A bicycle race were about to start:
I'm in the park, the sun is bright,
Water ravishes the eye, and soon
I've won the race, I've made my mark!
Then, once again, the telephone
Is my one lifeline out of the dark.

I'm sick of being obsessed by B.
Whose muffled cryptograms grow hoarse
Explaining themselves, outwitting me.
Does that mean this? Does this mean that?
Temperamental unclarity!

This week, drinks and dinner with M.
Lunch with L. Dinner with P.
A party for C.'s new Argentine.
Handel on Thursday. A *vernissage*.
Next week, drinks and dinner with M.
Tuesday I think I'll watch TV.

To retire from it all! To sit and sit
In a wheelchair, old, in Central Park,
Only a lens that drinks the sun,
Or on a bench in southern France,
The first cassis at four o'clock. . . .

August was green, November brown.
Someday soon I'll awake to see
The world go white from head to toe,
A tablecloth at first, and then
A slab of pockmarked travertine—

The first snow.

From New Poems *(1971)*

Ménage à Trois

Another sunset of scrambled eggs
And wine, Mars under the piano, laughing,
Venus at the door of the frigidaire,
Saying, "We're all out of blood again!"
How I deplore her use of the language!
You ask how we get along? Not well.
Temperamental discrepancies:
Her habit of saying nothing grandly,
His fake interest in the cause of things.
The food is dreadful. The weather worse.
So much for all the touted joys
Of the Riviera—or wherever we are.
The dullness of the nights is hard to believe,
Though, from outside, I gather we cause
A sensation. Who's sleeping with whom?
We keep them guessing: Nobody is.
The schedule goes something like this:
She works on her cookbook, "Venus Cooks,"
He works part time at the Peace Foundation.
And I start out—well, you know me:
I rip through the Debussy Preludes, shave,
Feel ashamed at detesting travel,
Read, write, go for a walk, and think—
Not that there's much here to think about.
Lunch, usually mushrooms picked
By the local mushroom maniac, whom
We trust, *ça va sans dire*, then back
To my desk for a note or two, more work,
He comes home, she *in* from the gazebo,
Where she writes—and then it's cocktail time!
Singapore slings served in jelly glasses,
Both à la mode in nineteen thirty-nine
(That's the year the Spanish War closed down).
To say I was bored would overstate the case.
I'm languid. They're worse. Desultory.

Of course, he's nineteen, and has fresh thoughts,
She *can* be amusing. At dusk, on the terrace,
I get myself up like a Chinese sage,
My bathrobe from Brooks dyed raven blue,
And we talk of our Oedipal strangulations—
Each so different and each the same.
Later, we provide pornography
(Mental) for the neighbors, who watch our blinds
As if they were about to disclose an orgy,
Something worthy of the TV sets
They hunch over like a herd of cattle.
Then, with a little citrus kiss goodnight,
We part, and so the days go by. . . .

We're followed to the market by a limousine,
Green, a Rolls, in which an assassin
Is discreetly invisible in the back seat.
So we say. It's probably the victim.
I have come to believe in loneliness,
Disguised as it is as an optical illusion.
Rumors are rife: something rose from the sea,
Somebody saw a stain of blood—
But, no matter what they say, the sun's the same.
This morning, I wrote, beginning a poem,
"That sedative, the sun"—but I couldn't go on.
They're at the door. Another game.
She: (Screaming) "Leave me *alone!*"
He: "Tonight, we'll really go to town."
You want my view of the whole situation?
It's old, inadequate, and flourishing.

The Hand

I have watched your fingers drum
Against each other: thumb against
The fore- and middle-finger. When
Tension leaves your hand alone,
Your face slides back its screen, I see
Such streams begin, such gardens grow
That you must hide more than you hide,
And I must know more than I know.

Radical Departures

Money on the snake   they couldn't stay
There was an end   in Eden   to small talk
That was the first departure   chalk on black
Memoranda   were not so in May

When sin and plaything   were transfigured by
Some dandelion child   with a tin can
Who painted badly   the afternoon
Owed something   more than something   to the sea

But then, who doesn't?   Any shady warehouse
Crammed with the used-up   failures of one life
Proves lifeboats aren't safe   a rusty knife
They cut you up   they screw you   take my advice

It's gloomy   the truth hurts   *c'est dommage*
I've had enough   of voyages and moons
Zebra boardwalk lights   and painted signs
Misdirecting me   like This Garage

Is Open   and then twenty yards away
We're All Filled Up   Get up, go out to Queens
Preferably on a Sunday   when it rains
And take a look at   any cemetery

Jammed with a traffic jam no two-bit crook
Appointed the   Commissioner of Traf-
fic ever fought his way through for the tariff
And when they book you   they throw the whole book

At you   at me   at us   I'm talking about
Radical departures   Jim shot himself
This morning   awful   Eloise and Ralph
Took pills   And Sissy swam the long way out

And around   gin, bourbon   dear alcohol
Always does the trick   Mirrors never lie
Even distorted ones   like Our Old Family
Album   whose dumb positives recall

The negatives behind   the black and whites
Go out to Queens   and take a look around
Highrisers   brick   carefully rezoned
Pile ugliness on ugly   Civil Rights

Are getting much less civil   Citizens!
If General Torture, Inc. could have its way
Nothing of memoranda   would be May
It's Can   and Do   Do you remember trains?

Sure I remember trains   I went to Maine
Once   It took a pig to cross the line
At Chicago   You'd better take the plane
Be careful   smoking grass   the main line

Don't mention love   my God   or self-esteem
Quality products   now produced by Thug,
Inc.   The chances aren't good   a bug
Crossing the Atlantic   on a stem

(Interruption: "In colored slides   I'll show
Without a doubt   how each biography
Clean as a whistle on top   is a dirty
Lie at the bottom   and, blow by blow. . . .

And other unnatural practices which
Made public   can do a senator in
Real quick   which also goes for everyone
Keep your nose clean   though no one here, natch,

Has anything to fear." At which the screen
Was lowered,   the shot rang out,   and, stunned,
Everyone stared down   at the auto-gunned
Governor   who fell for an ex-Marine.)

The girl from Ipanema   night and day
Won't you do, do, do   all the things you are
This guy's in love with you   eight to the bar
One o'clock jump   after you   take the A

Train   you'll never get from here to there
They're on a yacht   the wine Aegean's prose
Integrate the schools   said Old Man Mose
The Wasp said   The Jew and Negro share

A common fate   Let *them* ask the reasons
One's black   one's white   It's *their* funeral
I think you'd better vote for me, you all
Intellect at bay   the fate of nations

Goodbye   The thrilling thing to be is stark
Naked   it gets a laugh each time   time is
On time   eats lion   lamb   it's famous
And so is what the dark does to the dark

Where the Castle Is

The upkeep of the castle is
The downfall of the cottages
Where fishermen and peasants live
Or used to live. The young men leave
In homemade boats in which they drown,
In makeshift planes that burn and crash,
Or die of boredom on the train
That starts each month for Cold Cash,
Only to find when they arrive
That that's not where the castle is.

The women left live in the sticks,
And when they do the weekly wash
Or mend the nets to catch the fish,
They sing this song: "We work for weeks
For nothing. Now the men have gone,
We'd like to be where money talks,
For all the rest is gibberish."
They pack their bags and take the train
And travel through a strange terrain,
But not to where the castle is.

When there's no one left but children
And the very old, the young
And lame survivors play a game
Invariable in its details
In which they take the daily trash
Down to the dump and sing a song
About ash heaps and burials
Whose burden always is the same:
"If we were old, if we were young,
We'd find out where the castle is."

At Cold Cash, where the castle is,
Or where it is supposed to be,
Nobody ever dies, it seems;
They just go on—from first to last
A series of monotonies—
And they play bridge, mah-jongg, and gin
The while they sing their tribal song,
Which has no verse but a refrain:
"We're here. And if we're here, of course,
This must be where the castle is."

But even kings get sick and bank
Accounts go bad and miracles
Occur, though sometimes in reverse;
Elaborate discrepancies
Narrow down from bad to worse;
Abysses open in a wink
Below the shining pinnacles—
"We do not know the place," they sing,
"That once we thought the castle was.
Do you know where the castle is?"

They travel near, they travel far
To seek out where the castle is,
And come upon the cottages,
Which lie in smoking ruins, and there's
No man alive, no woman now
To point the way, and though they sift
Through the debris and pan the clay,
Searching for the smallest clues,
They haven't found out to this day
Just where the castle was, or is.

The Advisers

Fine print gone dim,
The night's blind crone made much of her and him,
But they, not reading braille,
Awoke, at dawn, untutored still,

And pulled their weight
Across the fetid waters of the strait
Till, stranded on the bar
Of time at last, they saw that far

Was near. They said,
"Mirrored in us you'll find yourself." Dead,
I thought. A bad mistake
Ever to have come. Though that week,

And much later,
Reading between the lines in my own mirror,
I heard the clock persist,
As self-love does, dying to exist.

Long Island Springs

Long Island springs not much went on,
Except the small plots gave their all
In weeds and good grass; the mowers mowed
Up to the half-moon gardens crammed
With anything that grew. Our colored maid

Lived downstairs in a room too small
To keep a bird in, or so she claimed;
She liked her drinks, sloe-gin, gin-and . . .
When she was fired, my grandma said,
"Give them a finger, they'll take your hand."

So much for the maid. My grandma lived
In a room almost as small. She gave
Bread to the birds, saved bits of string,
Paper, buttons, old shoelaces, thread . . .
Not peasant stock but peasant—the real thing.

What stuff we farmed in our backyard!
Horseradish that my grandma stained beet-red—
Hot rouge for fish—her cosmos plants
With feathery-fine carrot leaves, and my
Poor vegetables, no first class restaurant's

Idea of France. "Your radishes are good,"
My sister said, who wouldn't touch the soil.
My mother wouldn't either. "Dirt, that's all."
Those afternoons of bridge and mah-jongg games,
Those tournaments! Click-click went forty nails

That stopped their racket for the candy dish.
"Coffee, girls?" came floating up the stairs.
Our house was "French Provincial." Chinese mirrors
Warred against the provinces. The breakfast nook
Had a kind of style. But it wasn't ours.

I'd walk down to the bay and sit alone
And listen to the tide chew gum. There was
An airport on the other shore. Toy-like,
It blew toy moths into the air. At night,
We'd hear the distant thunder of New York.

Grandpa, forgive me. When you called for me
At school in a sudden rain or snow, I was
Ashamed that anyone would see your beard
Or hear you talk in broken English. You
Would bring a black umbrella, battle-scarred,

And walk me home beneath it through the lots,
Where seasonal wild roses took a spill
And blew their cups, and sumac bushes grew
Up from the sand, attached to secret springs,
As I was secretly attached to you.

Friday night. The Bible. The smell of soup,
Fresh bread in the oven, the mumbling from
The kitchen where my grandma said her prayers.
Reading the Bible, she kept one finger under
Every line she read. Alone, upstairs,

The timelessness of swamps came over me,
A perpetual passing of no time, it seemed,
Waiting for dinner, waiting to get up
From dinner, waiting, waiting all the time.
For what? For love, as longed-for as a trip

A shut-in never takes. It came to me.
But what Proust said is true: If you get
What you want in life, by the time you do,
You no longer want it. But that's another
Story, or stories, I should say, much too

Pointless to go into now. For what
Matters to me are those lifelong two
Transplanted figures in a suburb who
Loved me without saying, "I love you."
Grandpa, tonight, I think of you.

Envoi:
Grandma, your bones lie out in Queens.
The black funeral parlor limousines
Just make it up the narrow aisles.
When flowers on your headstone turn to moss,
Russian cossack horses leap across
The stone, the stone parentheses of years.

The North Sea

1

Ask the North Sea to have a heart.
Few have touched it. It feels nothing.
You will be met by gray-steel bays
Terraced with ice, a frozen spittle
Of spray, and a long monotonous sound
Not quite distinct from silence. For
The naked eye: glacial resorts
Of black and blue, a few bleak windows,
Wicks of the sun on rock, and thin
Birds going over, searching for food.

2

Ask again. What you know you know
Is not what you feel. A sudden concussion
Of ice throws up its treasured bits,
A handful of jewels pressed quite clean.
Miles away, through binoculars,
Moribund waiters hobble across
The awninged porch of a rich hotel.
Far out, where the water is still moving,
.We call and deliver, the buoys sing.
But to whom and what they do not say.

3

This place is not in love with you.
That only makes you love it more.
It is as clever as can be,
It can advance and then withdraw.
It is something you cannot know
But want to badly. It has no heart
But needs one desperately. Through you,
It hopes to learn to play its part,
Even perhaps to *be* you—though
Then, of course, it would bore you stiff.

4

The consolations of alcohol
Or drugs might help to pass the time—
Not that either is available.
Before long, you may sit and stare
At nothing, the flora of this place,
At semblance, the fauna of the world.
Pure science is corrupted by
Pure cold into a literary form
As dangerous as the cancer of
The south. And you begin to dream.

5

You dream the moment's sustenance
Is working against all error, hands
Hand you back your heart all healed.
The set goes dark. You're somewhere else:
You're in the center of a bad idea,
You're in the mind's stupid studio
Filled with inferior art. You're in
That mockup of a powder room
Where skeletons make up. One says,
"Ask the North Sea to have a heart."

6

You wake. And think there used to be
A railroad here. There must have been.
The tracks are gone. Where did it go,
That train that used to go between
Here—and where? Moscow? Rome?
No one has heard of either place.
No one is here to hear of them.
If you could leave for somewhere else,
Preferably in the Temperate Zone. . .
The sounds of the whistles increase. The bells.

7
A mirrored dread comes closer slowly
Dragging its wires across the snow.
It narrows the distance gradually;
It is watching you, yet it is you.
It opens its mouth to speak. Silence.
The mirror begins to melt and bleed.
No music warms the baleful vision,
No voices charm the unbearable.
The desired and dreaded arrive at once,
Their true proportions coming clear.

From Buried City *(1975)*

Chekhov

We have the whole evening ahead of us,
We think, our eyesight starting to weaken,
We must have missed the houselights growing dim,
But how could that moment have escaped us when
The roots of the paper trees struck water
And transformed themselves into the real thing—
This nervous wood at the edge of a small,
Provincial town whose still lifes waken
To find that they're portraits after all
And subject to the risk of animation?

Tonight we may discuss—after the Chopin
Nocturnes, after the I-don't-know-how-many
Performances of Beethoven's "Moonlight" Sonata—
The gradual reduction of Roman columns,
The disease of too many lakes and clouds.
Do cobblestones have a future? Is rain
Removeable? Depressing mornings find
Characters in bed who have no reason
To get up, the light a yellowish half-light
Mirroring the mind, its sad affections.

At the lake, a flat of faultless summer
Is being taken down, the view abandoned;
The puzzled players change their places. Once
You might have found them walking in an orchard,
The blossoms opening their mouths to speak
And song occurring as if it were natural;
Now that trees uproot themselves and bankrupt
Agriculture wanes in its drying furrows,
Property and battlefields turn out to share
A fate in common—they exchange hands.

Shrines "fallen out of the perpendicular,"
Stones "that have apparently once been tombstones"—
We are on someone's estate not far from Moscow.
How simply the sun goes out like a match!
How deeply the wounds stay on the surface!
He said the best that can be said for property:
It lets an old man fall in love with landscape,
Lets so many trees have a chance to be noticed,
Allows the self-interested birds to preen,
Until the property is lost again

To an upstart creditor who sells the trees
For lumber, then, to the sound of saws,
Tramps through the hallway in his dirty boots
To explain, in tears, the dreary motivation:
His mother's dying, his young wife's in love
With a boor. . . . The Babel of trouble starts;
Among all the hells that go on talking,
Only one is real, though it is silent,
And everything leads up to it—to lose
The land, to lose the very ground you stand on.

If the temporary brilliancies gather once more
In the middle distance, and the modal lark
Persuades the summer evening to reveal
One private little splendor not for sale,
Still, a gunshot, onstage or off,
Tells us what no one is prepared to know:
Love is a tourniquet tightening its bands
Around the slowly dying wrist of freedom,
Futility's a spinster bending over
A book of household accounts forever.

Bathed in the acid of truth, all things
Become possible: to be a cold snake
At an interview, to live on scraps of soap
To keep oneself warm, to resemble a cat
Constantly stalking the shadow of nothing.
To the horse's clop-clop outside the window,
Or the sound of a guitar from a neighboring room,
The doctor, with a smile, asks, What is man?
A hero about to be done-in for good?
A villain about to be rescued by pain?

The governess is wearing her old forage cap.
That's Epihodov playing his guitar.
Astrov is talking about trees. We could be
Racing the wolves at thirty below
In a ravine whiplashed by snow, or slowly
Succumbing to boredom in a seaside town,
Waiting for a future that will never be,
The heat getting worse, far off the waves
Pounding faintly late in the moonlight,
At a low moment in our lives.

Someone

You watch the night like a material
Slowly being crammed into a tube of rooms;
It showers into gunshot, pepper, dew,
As if a hand had squeezed it at one end,
Is blank as innocence when daylight comes
Projecting sunlit patches on the wall
That fade. Too much is going on, too much
Of life, you say, for you to live alone
On top of an old tenement, on a train
That might start off sometime, but never does.
Your view is gone. Turn around, and boom!,
A park appears between two fixed ideas
Whose narrow aperture of sky in time
Will house the slums of 1989 . . .

Now New York is feigning its gray dark
London winter. Invisible uptown
Is out there somewhere, raining on its own.
Palmed in the dusty pane, a circle bares
A scene that seems reprinted from the past:
A man with a dog is walking very fast
Along a path among the stunted trees
Of the little square below. He disappears.

Winter Botany

1
You can hear the dogs
At the edge of town.
It's fall. The hills
Are slowly filling up with spinster sculpture—
Before the whole *mise en scène* collapses,
How can we explain our devotion to
The second rate,
Our three false languages:
Government, medicine, and law?

2
Who put those malteds in the sea
And the angels in alphabetical files?
The mail piles up for the departed,
The insipid surprises of middle life
Pile up, when what we wanted were
Tame lions with musicians in a royal park,
Extracts of smoke, the lunch of ages,
Undying moonlight fettered at the feet
Of prima ballerinas crammed with poems,
Whose net impact would be marvellous . . .

3
Instead what we got was a century
Good for poems but not for poets, talk
Reduced to small talk, grunts among the trees
Heralding the terrors of the lapsed thing:
Days whose events refused to happen,
Money lost before we could count it,
Nights of unrecollected being.

4

Night sweats and stomach cramps,
Their symptoms set the tone
In this city of four million love affairs
That has its night life on
And divides the world into two great camps:
The mad great, and the not great mad;
In dreams we find ourselves alone,
Looking down from a high wire,
With no net below,
Thinking we know one truth at least:
Not to be loved is to crave power.

Cold-Water Flats

A RAILROAD FLAT

The meanest melon slice of sunlight rims
An olive velvet unmade daybed, dims
Out of its own accord along the sides
Of a kitchen bathtub, hesitates, and then
Shivers for a second, and goes down the drain.
Two windows always face a tiny square
Of neon signs and grass—Hopper? Sloan?
Loneliness is like the upper floor
Of a house like this, where you live alone,
And downstairs somebody is always home.

TWO BAYS

A cardboard on its back, perforated by
A thousand little syphons, that's the bay—
Or was before the tide turned. Oysters caught
Their breath for miles around, and we caught them,
Bare-handed, barefoot, on cold-water flats.
That was Wellfleet. Now it's Gardiners Bay.
It's fishy here, and an unhappy place,
Or let's say we are. The fish factory's
Defunct. It squats like an abandoned town
That's lost its one and only industry.

WIND INSTRUMENTS

Sharps and flats. You need wind instruments
To play them, notes you never heard before,
Asleep between the strict piano keys.
They're lovelier than brains, what songbirds sing,
I mean blues singers singing after dark

Mid-Eastern scales through open windows—songs
That streak into the blood, are ready when
You least expect them on the sounding board,
And bring back taxi lights in rain, the inks
Of summer, its black lights, and golden tans.

WINDOWS

Another dumb enchanter out of gas,
I pass your house and look up in the dark;
You aren't home, or are asleep, I guess.
Blank bandages still waiting for their wounds,
The windows rise in tiers. As slow fog creams
Up from the river, sleepers turn their dreams
Into clichés come true. Who hasn't had
His private little hell? Oh, yes. Mine was
Those months of pain no one could see me through.
Not that you loved me. Or I loved you.

Tropical Fish

Velvet sulphur powder puffs, and cream
And lavender arrangements trimmed with ice,
Little chandeliers and pulsing lanterns,
Lipstick streaks, and ermined eyes of gin
Shaken in cut glass, and sleighs of Roman
Stripes, and azure mirrors under skin,
Bones like silk embedded in a crystal,
Armor made of mica, gilded wine
Strung like buoys along a throbbing wire,
Snows collecting into white jade bulges,
Milktails of successive pale blue arches
Stippling into gray, G-clef signs
Descending slowly on their licorice threading—
Glass and waterglass, rain on rain.

Sawdust

1

Open, doll. Switch off your golden hair.
Unzip the cross-stitched seam at the base there
And let the pale, crushed monitors float free.
Look at the empty wooden interior,
Solid but fragile, a fingernail of skull . . .
You can break it apart like a piece of candy.
Open, open up. Mr. Sesame is here,
Miss Thorazine in tight gold velvet tights,
And Thomas Edison, inventing night life—
Aren't they a winsome, gruesome threesome?
They clash, dash forward with their curving knives,
Circling toward the two bull's eyes ahead,
And out they go through two polestars of light.

2

Out to what? Did I say night life?
Septic dusk, the nets about to fall,
The silky excitement of a gypsy movie,
Magic cranked out of the ordinary:
Crowds—what crowds!—illusionary people!
Each, a silent telegram, goes by.
Satisfied hungers no longer suffice.
Here: two lovers translating each other.
Here: a schoolroom balanced on a cliff.
There: a street of epical negation—
Clothes that fall apart, food that cannot nourish.
(Only cheap places can pay the high rent now.)
The smog is trying to become more lucid.

3
Out of commission, gears mesh with anything.
Or rust. Sometimes it comes in cycles, say,
A little bit of both: frenzy and resting.
Violence pours from the vat of rejection
As if destruction were displaced affection.
Look at a tree. Then at the sawdust floor
Of one of those decorated, gimcrack places
That mimic the taste of the turn of the century.
Though you can't see it, you know the connection.
So get the matches and the needles ready,
The chains, the belts, the paraphernalia—
The bulging, red-eyed children plunge again
Into the powerless mirrors of power,
Still wondering, as the gearshifts move,
If pain is a substitute for love, or love.

At the Masseur's

1

Entering at first, body in mind,
I hadn't noticed the rug at all,
Its suède-green heron splayed against
Sky-blue, angora of light, a plush
Sand beach whose total afternoon
Unmitigated summer rocks with blue,
Savannas of weedy acres, winged
Needle-darters, nervous at the shore. . . .
This hallway's sensual stained red glass
In a leftover brownstone's leaded door,
My feet sinking into pile, I move
Obediently up the gloomy stairs.
Indoor pool? Cool funeral parlor?
Who else lay here, who else will lie?
The warp must go, all flesh is sand. . . .

I notice, body, you begin to end.

2

Undressed, pummelled, stroked, caressed,
What does the mind still grant to touch
Alone? Probably everything:
My nerves race backward through the years to one
Not quite recapturable afternoon
When power was in *my* hands . . . a green room
Of waves advancing, a chorus line
Of gulls, the shore's wet sand an ore
Dribbled like icing from a pastry tube
Onto the rising towers of a castle
The ocean crumbled. . . .
                              My body's struck anew
Under the studied cunning of a hand
Equally skilled at feather, silk, or steel.
Is this the stuff that Donatello knew,

Whose marble draperies could stir the wind?
Stone muscle, sinew, lion-limb that grew
Under the hands of Michelangelo?

Rodin! Your thinker is not thinking now!

The body's thirsting alleyways grow full
As pressure slakes them with its milk and dew:
Atlantic motion, Caribbean lull,
Beach umbrella, suntan lotion, shoe
Removed so foot may shape itself in sand,
Natural pleasure issues from the hand
Of . . .
  of a masseur who plays an instrument
Relaxed into the harp it meant to be,
And I, asleep upon the table, or
Dreaming it, emerging from the water,
Walk across the flashing yarns and edges
Of a carpet spread before the sea, whose border

3
Knits itself of thread,
Sinking foam, crêpe-paper,
Underfoot, instead
Of a heron a sandpiper—

The sheet is a sand beach,
That purring motor hum
Vibrator, tidal lurch . . .
Shaken, the waves come.

The body's second birth:
A Greek god Time undoes.
Now we are going north,
Landlubbers on a cruise,

To pines, lakes, motels;
Crawling through crumbling jade,
We snake up molded hills,
The late light lemonade . . .

In New Hampshire twilight
A swimmer streaks from shore
Out to his little float—
Square rug going threadbare . . . ?

One summer rectitude
Deserted me, half ill,
I took bread at the hand
Of a beggaring, sexual,

Illiterate command—
Bitter, obsessive summer!
Only flesh could mend . . .
Let's draw the veil of kind-

ly darkness over . . .

4
Slack and stress, first pressure and then none,
This life-saver revives his drowning man.
Aware of sound—a radio kept low—
I wake to see the curtains blow their cool,
A black cat pouncing on the daybed, my
White shirt a brand-new patchwork for its joy.

It's over. I get up. We talk. I dress.
A painting hangs beside an odd recess
That houses a small sculpture: *David*? No,
But something similar: a discus thrower
Last seen in grammar school. Poor Miss Lafour

Who mastered Art but not the art of dress . . .
The whole affair takes no more than an hour. . . .
I say I'll call again. Then pay. And go.

5
How much art hides! The varnish coats
Over the naked figure. Soon
Time takes them up, the rugs, the floats,
All places where the body's been.

"The figure in the carpet . . ." Henry James.
Time is at the loom. With a final stitch,
The design unravels. Memory blooms:
The past, the present. Who knows which is which?

To touch is to be touched. Maybe. Fleet
Fingers lead fleet lives. I see
At last the long drawn-out conceit:
Body. The sea. The Medici . . .

6
Kings have wept to know the frame of art
Is fleshless, soul lifting out of bone. . . .
Mind, you are singular, the heart stops
At the splendor of the young who all too soon
Drink up their ambience, eat out the heart
Of every age whose business is to kill
That sensual, that blushing animal,
So moving it seems more pure than all
The sculptors' moving hands, even when still.

The Stairs

Starting out as love, it climbed the stairs,
And then came down as something else again;
I did not recognize its killing features
Until I saw they were my very own.

Tonight, the babbling ghost of the remains
Sits in a room of starlight and of snow;
The owl tests its meretricious brains
Against the winter, and what comes back slow

Is the oldest sound that ever shook these hills,
The train's iron echo. Silence, its white bear,
States and restates a sentiment that kills:
Claws absolute. And plain. And everywhere.

Hair I remember, and lips like prizes,
The fluent eyes' divinities and, bare,
The flaring hollows of newborn surprises,
The clearest of all sleeps, then nothing clear.

Magic Affinities

The Muse disseminated wisdom's music:
"Three," she announced, "is the way of magic—
If you can arrange the same words three ways . . ."
                              George Tremplar

I

You, the lady of magic affinities,
Know how appetite grows larger on
What starves it. Such lovely days
Are lovely days for love, I could write,
And lie. Pleasures, complacencies,
Are habits remaining serviceable.
I am tired, yes. But not of you.

Evil arrives in the guise of the pitiful.
The dancers' synthetic intensity
Blurs the stony difference between
Desire and desire. Today the sea
Is filled with old Elizabethan plays . . .

Liar! The sunset's gravity reveals
Antonyms of green—sky-mirrors and delights,
The astrological swan, and others:
Sculpture, coliseums, coins, ourselves.
We were. We are. We will not be.
Each river has a town, each town a river;
Along its banks, it palms its treasuries:
Forms of knowledge, such as gravel, grass,
Sticks, stones, and light flotillas of the weed,
But, up in our houses, our nature is to fight
Nature.
        Lady, only arrive.

2

When we were complacent it was pleasureable,
But lady, that gravel is not grass on which
You bank your magic affinities
Grown larger on what starved them. I could write
We were ourselves the way the green takes light
Or rivers mirror towns, but evil arrives,
Blurring the difference between the sea
And the sunset. Remaining light reveals
The swan as a dancer of intensity
Whose antonyms—of gravity, delight—
Although synthetic, are still antonyms
Of coins whose serviceable habits lie,
Palmed treasuries in coliseum banks.

We fight the lovely days of love, and lie.
Desire is an old Elizabethan play,
A mirror of indifference because it is,
And was, and will be other than ourselves.
You know the sticks and stones of appetite
Are not the sky's astrologies but forms
Of knowledge. Flotillas of green grass
Fill up with towns of stone as we retire—
Pitiful sculptures housing our disguise.
Lady,
      nature only arrives.

3

Since tired nature is indifferent to
Coins, coliseums, Elizabethan plays,
And forms of knowledge, lady, arrive,
And be, like the astrological swan,
A magic affinity of appetite.

The sea is filled with sunsets and reveals
What largely starves us: the complacencies
Of habit—not the mirrors and delights
Of pleasure, but the lying sticks and stones
Of loveless days on lovely days for love.

The sea is stonily indifferent to
The otherness of blurred flotillas. We
Antonyms of nature are as weeds because
Our graves are natural and evil, yet
Green grass will house us and be serviceable.

The rivers' treasuries fight nature to
The sea; in stones, astrologies reveal
Their sculpturing, as if the sky, disguised,
Lay pitifully banked in gravel; palms
Remain along the river-banks, while towns

Grow starved on what enlarges them. When we
Dance, synthetic in intensity,
Starved on nature, starving on ourselves,
Delight may be sky-writing on the sky,
Lady,
        only nature arrives.

Hunting and Fishing

Who are you, love, who haunts the northern sphere?
Ghost of the shore, or lost desert walker,
Once flesh and blood, I took you in my arms,
The sheets turned over all their lakes and snows,
Four ungloved hands like hunters at their furs
No thicket overlooked, and no hedgerows,

Or, as the fisher over water goes,
We bent to bait the universal trout
Below, its silver scales our runabout;
Caught, pursuit ended, and ended travel
When breath sped blood to all its ports of call,
Angel who fell to nothing through a hole.

Bay Days

1

The clouds were doing unoriginal things
With grandeur yesterday, moving paintings
From here to there, slowly dispersing
Gangs of angels. Today there's nothing,
Nothing but a camera taking nothing.
Summer. Weather. Nothing could be clearer.
It is a perfect day, with no cloud cover.

2

The birds' gradual declensions stop.
The darkness takes the longest time to darken.
Sums of stars add to the overhead.
A city of hunches thickens and grows thin,
Appears and disappears across the water,
Depending on the light's strange gift for hanging
Scenery. And then for taking it down.

3

Each night, the outlines of that city form
Films of the ideal, illuminations
Of crumpled battlements whose rising argot
Is faintly heard above the motorboats;
Here, the night philosophers break camp
Down to a single-minded tent of parting.
The fire's out. The animals are gone.

4

Currents, always running, gauged to light
And wind, the depths varying the colors:
A copper milky green, an ink-splash blue
Turned tinsel. A vain castle's sinking
Into its sewerage system. A particle of sail,
Hurrying to meet its particle of sun,
Shakes the whole slack surface into speed.

5
Decisive laboring: the song recital
The rain was trying to compose this morning
On what the sun had glossed as marginalia.
References to happiness are obsolete
According to the gloomy view this evening,
Which says existence is the only share
Of ardent joy that's ever in our power.

6
I tried today to make of the wild roses
An untimely bouquet. Opening, falling,
They never last long—in short, they're dying.
Now I am thinking of taking to drinking
Earlier than usual. Gin. And something.
A potion of petals. They're thorns by evening.
Wild roses in the trash can in the morning.

Saratoga

Who would dream there is a street of Chasidic Jews
Left over among the mineral waters,
Black-bearded, black, among the cures of summer,
In rows of rooming houses gone to seed
Braced by vines in which they seem suspended?

This is a country of seconds—a kind
Of bucolic, demented Garment District:
Landscapes and yardgoods going for a song—
Windfalls of shirts on the cheap at the mill,
Factories where hands still touch the fabric.

The hills are overstocked with sunsets.
Cemeteries—are they housing projects
For never enough? Or too much of everything?
So this is the end of animals and dancers!
Poor brain, talking to a barn of dust!

In the dowdy beautiful Victorian dark
Of the steamy park's old brick and shadow,
Dilapidated concrete drowsy troughs,
Like laboratory tanks for mosquito larvae,
Piddle away brown-ferned scummed water.

How to be a beach resort without an ocean
Suggests the theme. The subject's certain:
The slower the town the more obsessed by speed.
Between the ballet dancers of July,
The dramatic, high-strung August chargers,

Surely some point must be being drawn!
Stirred up overnight: the swank emulsion
Of the rich, the corrupt, the merely sporting—
Dressy traders of expensive horseflesh,
Statues of jockeys upright on the lawn.

The Nineteenth Century is in the trees.
Down at the horse barns at night, the yearlings—
Part cricket field, part Arabian strains—
Wait to be named. Tradition . . . bargains.
Old tastes deplore the lost amenities.

Muscle under silk lifts the dancer's Swan,
Spurs the leggy velvet colt of speed—
Power gathered in the glacial rock fault
Tempting vision with what it cannot see:
Fresh water running toward immortal salt.

Shorelines

Someday I'll wake and hardly think of you;
You'll be some abstract deity, a myth—
Say Daphne, if you knew her as a tree.
Don't think I won't be grateful. I will be.
We'd shuck the oysters, cool them off with lime,
Spice them with Tabasco, and then scoop them up,
Who thought we were in Paradise. We were not.
Three couples and three singles shared that house
For two weeks in September. Wellfleet stayed
Remarkable that fall. And so did we.
Confessions, confidences kept us up
Half the night; the dawn birds found us still
Dead tired, clenched on the emotional,
Which led to two divorces later on,
Recriminations, torn-up loyalties,
The dreariness of things gone wrong for good.
Yet who could forget those wet, bucolic rides,
Drunk dances on the beach, the bonfires,
The sandy lobsters not quite fit to eat?
Well, there were other falls to come as bad,
But I still see us on a screened-in porch,
Dumbly determined to discover when
The tide turned and the bay sank back in mud.
We'd watch it carefully, hour after hour,
But somehow never could decide just when
The miracle occurred. Someone would run
Into the marshes yelling, "Where's the shore?"
We hardly see each other anymore.

Nearing the Lights

You are nearing the lights, either at
A window or on a road, you are
Watching the skyline right itself,
Or, coming into a town, you are

Watching the nearness somewhere else
Of early supper at a farm,
Or, in a town I'd never know,
Somewhere the lights are coming on,

Somewhere the night is holding out
And onto a river and a tree.
Is it the dusk or candlewick
Aflame or streetlamp that I see

Wavering, steadying, drawing near
Worlds that the day gives up to dark?
The moon puts down its gangplank in the sea
As if pure light could disembark.

Equivocal starlight turns into
Blank sky, then daylight. I see you
There at a window or in a car,
Where, in nearing the light, you are.

Buried City

If you have come, expecting miracles . . .
But you I need not warn. We worked for years
Only to arrive at deeper mysteries:
This cave, for instance, these rarities.
Notice the wall painting, strangest of all;
The hunter hunts himself, his animal—
Can you make it out, its pure illusion?

We've had it reproduced a hundred ways:
Reversed, blown-up, mirror-reversed, X-rayed,
Reduced, and so forth. Still we're in the dark.
And here, look close, an alphabet of shards—
Two perfect halves of shell, one broken one,
Intended, we believe, to signify
The pairings of the soul, the harm of love.

Some slanted stag—perhaps a buffalo
With horns above a human face, a spear
Pointing to its childlike heart and held
In . . . what? Paws? Fingers of a hand?—may be
A suicide at bay. Behind, a tree,
Half drawn to light and yet quite shadowy,
Proves the more we look the less we see.

And so the very subject of the painting still
Remains an enigma. I have stared at it
As if I were in love with its other side,
A silversmith inside a mirror, say,
Inventing winter, or a snowman turned
Into a figure-skater on the moon—
These icy images too soon give way

To tropical motifs: a diver in
A South Seas coral-blue lagoon—you know
Those afternoons we never think about

Until we're there in animal sunlight . . .
To be a diver and a scholar both
And not divided into north and south—
Could that be the painting's ambiguous myth?

Now we know that what we do not know
Stamps its print upon the brain in shadow,
A kind of Hegelian doubletalk
Has wrung the neck of all things straight. Behind
The mask its opposite, and so on. Where
The surface says all living things are one,
A deep disunity botches the design.

Imagine the rehearsals of the mad,
A stormswept gully where dead cats rain down
On peasants praying for food and water,
The inextinguishable pain of children
Destroyed by what can never happen. Think
Of houses, dinners, all mendacious calm,
Then, rising at the edge of Paradise, a slum

In whose bleak tenements some poor souls sit
Forever, staring into a machine,
Muttering about youth. A young girl, sick
At heart, keeps travelling through a town
Projected on a screen (of which she's unaware);
Trying to get to the other side each time,
And always failing, she begins again.

The painting is changing from this angle. Watch.
Among surrealist bits of paint and flame,
Coal barges burn themselves to water music,
Crass winter hazards clutter the spring stream,
Boats float past, reflected upside-down,

As if the malignant bridges of the town
Formed full circles—an optical illusion,

Along with many others. It's just one step
From the banquet hall to the garbage dump
And most of life takes place somewhere between.
We love high notes, expensive memories,
One more giant among the concertos,
Whose soloist needs rescuing from time to time
From heights on which he's suddenly stranded.

The sound of a light breather took us years
To trace, a joke of sorts too close to home;
At first the syllables were jumbled, words
Toppled on each other till we made them out:
Whispered art lectures, obscene taunts, and then
The sound of footsteps, running, running,
The breath of someone suddenly choked off.

Once more the threat of the internment camps,
Gas ovens, solitary pits, barb-wired
Fields, their blood-stained fences growing higher . . .
Psychology and history can't explain
Why power's cruel, and always was, and will be . . .
You name the one perfected revolution
Whose ends and means didn't separate in time!

The painting might symbolize the war between
Social classes, the ego and the id,
Black and white, the sexes, heart and spleen . . .
Or illustrate how God is territory,
Or could it be an ancient cryptogram?
An anagram of doubt—"You know . . . ?" "I mean . . . ?"
An early myth the shells were meant to story?

Prevailing easterlies, the winds that sit
In the hills beyond the roofs are ready to blow
Even this museum to salty pieces.
The sails rise up like salvaged laundry,
The cranks churn rust, and off we go again,
This time slightly askew, and slowly—
Only to be denied, once more, the harbor.

Baked in lava, the figures at Pompeii
Illustrated . . . what? Life becoming art?
Monogamous forever, coupled stone
Became pornography, a warning sign
To make ye haste, the rosebuds soon are gone;
Graffiti on the walls read *mene, mene,*
Tekel, upharsin—and the city fell.

And with it went the logs of fine apparel,
The rangy autumn days of walks and smoke,
The silver flanks of rock, the sulphur smudges
Floating on the bog's abandoned grasses
Housing a million forms of crawling life
That rose in gauze among the spring allotments—
Life so rich it oiled the hinge of feeling—

But when the city went, so did the country.
It's possible the painting is that world
Too soon pockmarked, diseased with furrows, or
Conversely mountained with the hilly scales
Of greasy patches of a sickness where
Beauty once had claimed a sure perfection—
Civil order crumbled into fiction?

Caveat emptor. Caves are everywhere:
Eye-pit, labyrinth of ear, skull-hollow,

Cavern of the grave. What appetite arouses
Pleasure defiles in age's tittle-tattle.
From here on in, we synchronize our watches,
For looking at paintings is a form of waiting
And time's the one disease everybody catches.

The wards of poverty remain the real
Real estate of history: Butchers share
Rooms at the top, those little royal roosts—
The King's chair here, the Queen's chair there;
Implicit hierarchies worked into the plan
Reveal the obvious: Envy, a small town,
Grew into the housing project of the world.

And yet that cemetery Valéry
Glazed into a permanent rooftop shimmer
Endures . . . but as a poem or a reality?
Even the truest of philosophies
Founders on the death of the philosopher.
The sea's a grave. A graveyard at the sea
Occasions, and subverts, the poetry.

Slowly this buried city came to light.
Up from the ruins, all its riddles blank
(Its verses, too), with no one to look out
While all of us looked in. We were the mere
Observers, really, not the partisans
Of life. At the exit, sign the pledge
Forbidding you to say that we exist at all.

Let them not wash in the wake of the uttering
Seagulls or blind themselves white on embankments
Of chalk or devour the dry egg of madness . . .
Words dimly scribbled on the wall revive

A city in the brain, its choked canals,
Its crowded terminals . . . We're rising through
Levels of thought where dark and light converge.

And now the World . . . We've reached the upper air.
Goodbye, goodbye . . . The deer stop dead to hear
The first retort of gunshots in the wood.
Exiled from exile, you will always bear
Two sacred marks of the interior:
Memory and art. How early it grows dark!
They say the snow will bury us this year.

From A Swim off the Rocks *(1976): Light Works*

A Swim off the Rocks

A flat rock is the best for taking off.
    Rafferty, the lawyer, with a cough,
        Goes first, head first—a dive
That makes us wonder how he's still alive!
    The ballerina's next, and shames us all.
What grace in space! What an Australian crawl!

I'm next—and too self-conscious to be good.
    When I look back to where I stood,
        Miss Jones, a leather crafter,
Has run, jumped in, and made it to the raft. Her
Body salty-white, she stares back at the shore, a
Lot like Lot's wife in Sodom and Gomorrah.

The ballerina knows how much restraint
    Enhances skill and, with a little feint,
        Spins away. Now Rafferty
Appears to be arguing a case at sea.
Splashing, gesticulating, he swims back,
And climbs, exhausted, onto the rock.

Miss Jones comes in—martyred, ill at ease,
    And towels carefully, even knees,
        While the lawyer fetches beer.
The dancer always seems to disappear.
Miss Jones, sotto-voce: "It's *said*, in *town*,
She's found a choreographer all her own."

What *I* say, though, is let what *is* just be.
    Miss Jones and Mr. Rafferty—
        A hopeless combination—
Have my good wishes for a grand vacation.
The dancer needs no help, evidently.
And as for me, I simply like the sea.

Tourists

Cramped like sardines on the Queens, and sedated,
The sittings all first, the roommates mismated,

Three nuns at the table, the waiter a barber,
Then dumped with their luggage at some frumpish harbor,

Veering through rapids in a vapid *rapido*
To view the new moon from a ruin on the Lido,

Or a sundown in London from a rundown Mercedes,
Then high-borne to Glyndebourne for Orfeo in Hades,

Embarrassed in Paris in Harris tweed, dying to
Get to the next museum piece that they're flying to,

Finding, in Frankfurt, that one indigestible
Comestible makes them too ill for the Festival,

Footloose in Lucerne, or taking a pub in in
Stratford or Glasgow, or maudlin in Dublin, in-

sensitive, garrulous, querulous, audible,
Drunk in the Dolomites, tuning a portable,

Homesick in Stockholm, or dressed to toboggan
At the wrong time of year in too dear Copenhagen,

Generally being too genial or hostile—
Too grand at the Grand, too old at the Hostel—

Humdrum conundrums, what's to become of them?
Most will come home, but there will be some of them

Subsiding like Lawrence in Florence, or crazily
Ending up tending shop up in Fiesole.

A Song Struck from the Records

Dear fairy Godmother, hold back
    Your magic transformation;
I see a coming cul-de-sac
    In rising above my station:
I know my clothes are awful, my
    Room a mess, but then,
At least I'm not surrounded by
    Secret Service men.
I fear the Prince's hunting lodge,
    I fear, my dear, his mother;
Frankly, I hate the whole hodgepodge,
    And the infernal bother.

No Prince falls short of the ideal
    Except on close inspection,
And royal houses, once they're real,
    Reveal some imperfection:
The widest moat, so crystal clear
    Today, becomes tomorrow
A muddy ditch with scummed veneer,
    Incredibly more narrow.
I'd be, should you invoke your wand,
    More sinned against than sinning,
And sadder at the happy end
    Than at the sad beginning.

Hansel and Gretel

To be baked as cookies by the mad witch?
Not so funny. See *The Rise and Fall
Of the Third Reich*. What starts out as kitsch
All too soon becomes a form of evil.

The witch was wise. What sweet tooth can resist
A candy cottage? They were wiser still,
Scattering their breadcrumbs not to get lost.
How could the witch know that they were trained to kill?

They got back home all right, the cunning children,
Only to end up in Munich, years later,
Stirring up the witchcraft of their own cauldron,
She a drunk and he a sadistic waiter.

"Maybe it would have been better," she said,
One day in her cups, "to have roasted in the oven
Than to hobble around this city, half dead—
Old movie stars in some dreary love-in."

At which he struck her. "Peasant . . . *peasant!*"
Then, lunging toward her, "You ungrateful bitch!
I wasted my life on our stupid legend
When my one and only love was the dead witch."

Fern Dying

I left it in the mailbox an entire day,
The latest note from Madame Blank who writes,
"Expect nothing, dear. You won't be disappointed."
I read it wolfing down my frozen dinner
Tasting so full of chemicals it might
Well be a form of dry shampoo reshaped,
How cleverly! into this turkey loaf
I scrape away—to join its chef, I hope.

I walk outside onto the moonless terrace.
Conservatory sounds: FM, TV,
The new urban music—gunshots, sirens,
Air-conditioners, exhausted, vented . . .
How sad the lighted trees in these environs!
If they could make a wish, they'd be transplanted

—And so would I.

        A Francophile whose style
Is the ultimate Morse Code in dots and dashes,
Madame underlines her words for emphasis:

"Here are my versions of some René Char
Poems . . . Be *frank*! *Tell* me—are they *good*?
Or *bad*, as the case may be! Don't spare
The rod! And here's my essay on Cocteau
(We were too *close* for him to mention me . . .)—
It's *still* unpublished! Tell me . . . *really*! *Why?*"

And so on. So forth. Blah, blah. Then,
Ending with a postscript *interruptus*:

"Goodbye, my dear, until we meet again . . .
I trust I can count on an *early* opinion? . . .
I'll call on Wednesday to arrange just *when* . . ."

On my desk my Boston fern is dying
From rot or heat, brown-leaved, tobacco-tongued,
Too dry, too wet, impossible to know . . .
Sometimes I wish that plants would find their voice
As I've found mine, coaxing one to grow;
I've sung to it, addressed it with commands
Brown thumbs resort to trying to be green—
Bloom! Bloom! Like Molly in *Ulysses.* Joyce.
A spore is not a flower. Jean Cocteau?

I sound like Madame Blank. I mean between
The lines . . . Or in them. That old pathetic bore!
That dying generation with no song!
And with that, unexpected tears. Poor lady!
Poor fern! The room is gravid with self-pity.
My ballpoint pen is writing something:
                                        "Dear
Madame Blank,
            Wednesday will be fine . . ."

Short Stories

"Lover, you are the child I will never
Have . . . *have* had . . . *will* have," she wrote.
That was in Denver. October or November.
Long before she married a lawyer.
They're living, now, unhappily forever.

   He was writing in Greece, and from:
   " 'In the time it took not to get to the castle,
   Space developed its chronic asthma . . .'
   I'm fleeing with the cat to Hydra.
   Escapes and such have gorgeous results.
   I'm giving it up. Can't write at all.
   So long. And scratch one nightingale."

If you climb to the top of a bank building
In Denver, the highest one around,
All you can see for miles are mountains.
Banks and insurance companies have
The money to build and build and build.
"The *hell* with architecture," he said—
A trustee of The Wheat and Bread
Amalgamated Holding Co.—
"Get a contractor. And let's go."
His wife was home, drinking again.
She thought: I mustn't forget to eat.

   "It is the dumb, intractable
   Retarded who are sexual
   And hold the mystery in their hands . . ."
   A professor wrote, after his class.
   Revised, rewritten, then recast
   Into the form of a Gothic novel
   About a nun who meets the devil,
   Bewitches him—the usual *kitsch*—
   Half put-on and half spiritual,

It sold over a million copies
And made the professor very rich.

Meanwhile, a thousand miles away,
On a bulletin board at IBM's
Six hundred thousandth factory,
The following message found its way:
"If anyone hears of a small, unfurnished
Air-conditioned person . . ."

"Children, you are the lovers I
Could never get," she almost said
Under her breath, which was just as well
Since it was nine-tenths alcohol.
"It's time for another drink, I guess.
Yes? . . . No. . . . No? . . . Yes."

In Greece, he started to write again,
"The Underground Sonnets" in four-beat lines:
"And I would find it hard to say
Who went where and who which way,"
Interrupted by the arrival of
One of the Greek hoodlums of love . . .

The following month his editor wrote,
"*An*drew, *what* is *hap*pening to you?
You know the ms. is unpublishable . . ."

The professor, after his first success,
Went back to poetry. Which did not, alas,
Return the compliment. And so he wrote
A book of comic meditations
Filched from sources not hard to trace.
He was saved by tenure and an understanding
Dean, spent six weeks at a *place*,

Where everyone was nice but the nurses.
The doctor said, "It's no disgrace . . ."

In Denver, the hotel bar's discreet.
A layman (ha ha) would never know
What's going on, it looks so straight.
After it closes . . . *you* know . . .
A little car on a back street,
And so forth.

"People aren't really built to stand
The kind of tension you get these days;
Betrayal in personal relationships
Is the very worst, of course, because
The Oedipal syndrome is revived again . . .
I think that guilt, not fear's the thing
For which we pay the highest cost;
I, personally, find it hard to feel
Guilty—except at not feeling guilt . . ."

The professor listened but wasn't cured
And produced that long, astonishing book,
*Counting Sheep or The Shepherd's Crook:
Deviation on the Western Plains,*
Which has just come out as a paperback
With an introduction by a poet back
From Greece . . .

She read it in a nursing home,
Having arrived at the same place
The professor recently left. And soon
They dried her out and sent her home.
She's fine in public now "but not
So hot in bed," the trustee said—
The trustee of the Wheat and Bread.

"One more poem, one more try,"
The prof to the poet said, whose sly
Rejoinder was, "With me, it's vi-
ce versa . . ."

One night, back on the sauce, she said,
Looking the trustee straight in the eye,
"*You* are the death I would never have,
I *thought* . . ."

The message on the bulletin board
Has had several replies, but none
Satisfactory. And yesterday
It disappeared. Or was thrown away.

The End of Words:
An Election-Year Thought

Drive past in the night; the two white lions
Of the library crouch, quite unaware
Of deficit financing, of literary lions
Working the moonlit salons of uptown
Going downhill fast. And so it's time
To fall in love with the first lip reader
You meet, avoiding the ever-present falseness
Of language. What will there be left to read?
Nothing. Yet it's better than pretending
Those deadly cackles are some form of speech,
To go on speaking, endlessly defending
Feelings never felt, words now dead,
Distorted, or misused. Other suggestions:
Writing poems in math, pressing flowers
Between blank pages of a book, or finding
Manuscripts among our future ruins
Untranslated from the original Garbage,
That tongue that power captured for the world
Which is now the only utterance of statesmen.

Charm

Intelligence endures
The sea-shake of the heart,
Its flops and opening nights,
But the body's theatre alone
Eludes even its playwrights:
Too soon the script is done,
The curtain down. Applause.
Bravo! Encore! The lights . . .
And a rush to the doors.

Because the world's police
Have instinct on the books,
Innocence is nice
But not for long. Good looks
Turn bad, and time's as famous
For playing dirty tricks
As virtue is, whose price
Is beautifully to skate
On increasingly thin ice.

The beauties of the brain
And body are not charm—
Though charming they can be.
Charm is a sympathy
That sometimes draws a line
Under the unProfound
By an irony of tone,
And it is mostly missed
Once it is heard and gone.

Old bones know charm the best;
They see the trees for the wood,
The shades at their light task,
The magical latitude
That time cannot redress;

Their knowledge is their loss:
Under the worldly mask
They take off at their risk
They feel the pull of childhood.

Life adds up to not much.
Subtracted every day
Another sparrow falls
Oblivious from its perch.
That truth lacks charm, it's true,
Directly looked at, but
There is that version which
Can sometimes sound the depths
With the lightest touch.

The Refrigerator

The argument of the refrigerator wakes me.
It is trying to tell me it doesn't want to be cold,
It never wanted to be cold, it didn't choose
This life where everyone around it hates it.
"People only use me for their own convenience,"
It says. With a shudder, it starts off again,
Undergoing an electrical seizure,
Rambling on about its hurts and troubles:
People think it's heartless, stolid, frigid,
When, deep down, it craves for warmth and wants . . .
Well, it hesitates to say it, but
All it *really* wants is to be a stove.
Oh, how it dreams each night of the paired
Gas jets switching on their tropical blue,
The swoosh just after the match catches on,
The rectangular, passionate grid of flame
In the oven, the romance of changing things
Into other things. "The egg of the Real
Becoming the soufflé of the Ideal—
That's what I call the creative life."

"You perform an important function," I say,
"Without you, where would we be, these days . . ."
"Yes, yes, I know," it impatiently replies,
"But do you"—pause—"think I'm attractive?"
My silence, I fear, gives the show away.
"Of course," I stumble on, "for what you do,
You're remarkably well made, so few things work . . ."
Coldly, it opens, then slams its door.
"I didn't mean . . ." I say. But it will not respond.
At midnight, with a premeditated click,
It detaches itself from the circuits of the world,
Manages to shut itself off completely,
And gives up the ghost. By morning, all is lost.
"Damn it," I say to my coffee, black

(The milk's turned sour overnight),
"Unfulfillment's claimed yet another victim,"
Just as the stove speaks up to say,
"Do you think? . . . I hear . . . in the frozen north . . ."

Circle

Now are we saying goodbye?
I think so but can't be sure.
The last phone call but one
Left everything up in the air.
When you called last, did you mean
What you said when you said you meant
To say that this call would be
The last if I didn't call?
In fact, I'm not sure at all
If you called or I called you back.
And did you say "goodbye,"
Or I say "good night" and you
Say "Do you mean 'good night'
Or 'goodbye'?" I think it was you.
And what were you trying to do
When you said, "*You* said we're through?"
How could that be since you
Were the first to bring it up?
I don't think it's what *I* said,
Though you keep saying I did.
In any case, now that you know
That you know what I meant to say,
Why don't you say what you mean?
I mean if you mean to say
That the last call was the last.
I think that that would be best.
If something is finished, it's just
As well to get up and go.
If you're interested still to know,
I like a slate wiped clean,
And if you would pick up the phone,
I'd tell you what I mean.

Horror Movie

Dr. Unlikely, we love you so,
You who made the double-headed rabbits grow
From a single hare. Mutation's friend,
Who could have prophesied the end
When the Spider Woman deftly snared the fly
And the monsters strangled in a monstrous kiss
And somebody hissed, "You'll hang for this!"?

Dear Dracula, sleeping on your native soil
(Any other kind makes him spoil),
How we clapped when you broke the French door down
And surprised the bride in the overwrought bed.
Perfectly dressed for lunar research,
Your evening cape added much,
Though the bride, inexplicably dressed in furs,
Was a study in jaded jugulars.

Poor, tortured Leopard Man, you changed your spots
In the debauched village of the Pin-Head Tots;
How we wrung our hands, how we wept
When the eighteenth murder proved inept,
And, caught in the Phosphorous Cave of Sea,
Dangling the last of synthetic flesh,
You said, "There's something wrong with me."

The Wolf Man knew when he prowled at dawn
Beginnings spin a web where endings spawn.
The bat who lived on shaving cream,
A household pet of Dr. Dream,
Unfortunately maddened by the bedlam,
Turned on the Doc, bit the hand that fed him.

And you, Dr. X, who killed by moonlight,
We loved your scream in the laboratory
When the panel slid and the night was starry
And you threw the inventor in the crocodile pit
(An obscure point: Did he deserve it?)
And you took the gold to Transylvania
Where no one guessed how insane you were.

We thank you for the moral and the mood,
Dear Dr. Cliché, Nurse Platitude.
When we meet again by the Overturned Grave
Near the Sunken City of the Twisted Mind
(In *The Son of the Son of Frankenstein*),
Make the blood flow, make the motive muddy:
There's a little death in every body.

More Lives of the Great Composers

For, and after, Dana Gioia

I

Maurice Ravel would buy a bag of figs
and eat them greedily on his back porch
in St. Jean de Luz. His aunts were mortified.
"On summer nights great music drives me mad,"
said Richard Wagner to his maid. And yet
tonight across the street a piano plays
arpeggios of steel. On autumn days,
Schubert would work, then take a walk through woods.
Outside the snow is falling steadily,

and more's to come. A man goes by,
resembling Schubert in his great frockcoat
strolling through the autumn woods. Ravel
had relatives who almost drove him mad.
Tchaikovsky said, "If I could love a maid . . ."
In fact, he tried. The girl was mortified.
And yet across the street a piano plays
as if a madman on a summer night
were tearing down the stars on his back porch.

In the snow country, Bartok on a sleigh
rode toward a castle, and a plate of figs
lying on a table by the fire seemed
as fine as greatcoats seen through autumn woods.
Georges Enesco lost his Spanish maid.
"Go back to Barcelona—that back porch!
Ravel's 'Bolero' soon will drive you mad."
"Arpeggios of steel . . . I'm mortified"—
a Juilliard student. "Mine are soft as figs."

"The pentatonic scale? I do not give a fig
for it," Stravinsky said, but no one heard
because across the street a piano played
arpeggios of steel. "I'm mortified,"

said Mozart, "to find my summer nights
mistaken by the critics for a light snowfall."
Couperin felt, one autumn day, quite mad,
dreamt of his maid, and woke—"That poor old girl!"
"I regret nothing," said Maurice Ravel.

2

"Small talk isn't Ludwig's kind of thing,"
said Beethoven's nephew Karl to Meyerbeer.
Replied that jolly meister, "So I gather,"
though some say what he said was "So I hear."
"*Am* I doomed to be an orchestrator?"
asked Rimski-Korsakov. There was no reply.
"Such minstrelsy arises from the sea,
I think I'll orchestrate it." Claude Debussy.

"La Mer" revives the small talk of the sea,
its great-depth grandeur and its coast small beer.
"You take some jolly-meister orchestrator,
and play a Bach cantata for him, and you'll see
his face go blank with admiration. Me?
Oh, I rise early and stroll beside the sea,"
said Respighi to de Falla. There was no reply.
"I think I'll poison Mozart." Salieri.

Madame von Meck, writing to Tchaikovsky:
"Why don't I hear from you?" There was no reply.
Domenico Scarlatti walked beside the sea
and found the shoreline's foamy beer not jolly.
"Herr Goldberg, I'm feeling very sleepy." Bach.
"I am a great pianist." Paderewski—
"A good cadenza always makes me cry."
"I love the oboes' small talk." Offenbach.

"Sleepy, Herr Schumann?" asked Clara, softly—
she had a date with someone by the sea;
she played Chopin, then Brahms—three intermezzi—
to help along the sandman. There was no reply.
Said Proust to Debussy, "Though minstrelsy
arises from the sea—and *yours* is heavenly—
the world doesn't orchestrate our wishes neatly,
or so we gather as the years go by."

From Notes from the Castle
(*1979*)

Gravel

1

The many here
Are like those crossing
Rivers into exile, the many felled
In Mexico by the crossbows of Cortes,
The French falling in the Russian snows,
But none like these are constantly run over
By heavy wheels or suddenly shadowed
By heights it is impossible to fathom.

The most gentle of the small stones
Has fallen in love
With the ordinary flower beds of summer
Lying helpless till winter effects
The divorce of sunlit wood and violet,
The slow parting of shadow and hydrangea.

Among these dead, these small leftover
Fragments of something once colossal—
The glacier moving southward with its ice—

There is one lying in the path in stillness,
One awaking to a grand piano
Somewhere in the house,
Who is grappling inside the hard room of its head
With syllables, or a phrase of song,
All ears gathering to sound.

2

If you should hear
The sound of the rustling
Of fallen oak leaves,
Would it remind you
Of the wind in the upright
Bole of summer?

And would the upright
Oak tree remember
The mast of the green sail
High above it?

High above
The level
Of gravel?

3
Suppose they were countries,
Territories,
Each with its central
Intelligence, each
With its nucleus
Surrounded by matter,
And spilled from the flatbed
Of a truck
Onto a roadway,
Or hauled to a roof,
Afraid of nothing but tar.

4
They have laid down
The armor of the big stone
By being movable,
Their lichen and moss
Rubbed to nothing
By endless stormy
Crack divisions.

Today they are hit
By a steady rain;
Rivulets run
Between, connecting

The white and the brown one,
The gray and the blue one.

5
There is a line downtown
Which is the end of Italian ices

And the beginning of trading posts
In Chinatown. Not as definite

As edges that separate small stones,
It is unquestionably there,

There in a park where old men weigh
The Chinese young on trays of swing.

6
A foot at wrong angles
Shoots one under
The house
Into permanent black,

A hand flings one
Onto a field
Into the desert
Of sun forever.

7
To the ant
They are possibly boulders,

To the hawk
Nothing at all.

To themselves
They are always a mixture

Never to be singled
Out as one—

They yearn
To be made separate

Or to be part
Of some great thing.

They yearn
To be made solid.

8
These pebbles bristle. Whoever loves
The feel of nails could bed here forever
Stuck by the sharpest prickles of needles,
The flat blade and the serrated edge,
The pointed end, the ridges of hardness
Pressing in and hurting slightly
To stick in the sweating flesh of summer
Till somebody mad for a coldsuit of water
Might lie in the heat of an August driveway
Covered from head to foot with gravel,
Rolling this way and that in a fever.

9
Bone of a leaf
On stone,

You are the smallest
Lithograph.

10
Whatever has been taken out
Will be put back,
The drawers filled again
With their pressed clothes,
The organs of the body
Folded back whole,
And the shell underfoot,
Inadvertently broken,
Reassembled
With every flute of the scallop
Intact, and be placed
In its place in the glass
Container, and
The wings of the moth
Singed so the body
Spiralled in flame
Will arise anew
To be healed again,
To achieve again
Its rise and fall,

So the name of the thing
Will be truly the thing,
And stone
Will be more than stone.

Notes from the Castle

The sunlight was not our concern or even
The pane it shone through, and no one was going
Down for the mail, and the four lettuces
The gardener brought as a gift seemed to be
A calculated bounty, so that early on
We knew we were going to be stuck with ourselves
The rest of the day, the vicissitudes
Marching in rows from the forest, the balms
Not arriving till nightfall. On the prowl
Since morning, the wind had a touch too much
Of motivation, an annoying way
Of exactly ruffling the same oak leaf
As if it were practicing a piano trill;
All day, repetitive birds, far off,
Were either boring themselves to death
Or, drunk on instinct, doing their thing:
Ritual dances, territorial rites—
The whole imperial egg. What nests
Ambition is weaving in us is hard
To say: after the flat occasion,
The unshared sphere, each childish wish
Grows hopeless finding this is what the world is.
For this, the recommended cures are useless:
A cheery hello to the disaffected
At breakfast? A soupful of tears at dinner?
You could spill the whole silly story out
To one more demanding, ill-tempered beauty
You happened to meet at the A. & P.,
And still every greedy shopping cart,
First overstuffed and then abandoned
In the parking lot, would leave in its wake
Some human need, ignored, half-starved . . .
Torn between having nothing to say
And saying it, whole diaries get down:
How terrible to have dressed beautifully for the rain! . . .

I was launched on New York's bisexual muddle . . .
And so on. And always the hoped-for redeemer
Turns up and turns with a country stare:
The girl in the lime linen shorts, the boy
With blond corn-silk tow hair, the heart
Speeding up until they speak: the dross
Of cars, the sportsman's life, and money;
And so, believing that you had come
To rest among the innocent soldiers
Of sleep, you had merely stumbled on
Another temporary battlefield
As never-lasting as the shine of water.

The Night Express

That moment we neared the reservoir
Dry wit dried up aware that water
Was no longer there for the taking. Hazel
And birch, those secret, solitary drinkers,
Were suddenly duplicated everywhere,
Even the ground consuming its potion.
The word on every lip was "parched."
Could the desert be a stone's throw away,
As so many people had guessed? In her bath,
The old lady down the road was appalled
To find herself knee-deep in rust:
This after years of a limpid clearness,
Soap beautifully wrapped and scented—
It was better than a sojourn at a thousand spas.
The sodas of the springs, the dew
Knew they were doomed not to be, feather-
Bedders of a union that had seen its day.
And so moisture, morning mist, and streaks
Of rain became so valuable collectors
Held out cans especially designed
To catch every drop of the cold sweat
Of the night express as it went roaring by.

At the Café

At the café, at an outdoor table
Fronting the last of the puppet shows,
We have come to sip a bit of brandy
And watch the rapidly descending evening.
Violinists scrape the bow of air,
Arguments begin and finish soon,
As if philosophy were running a café
Where nothing is served but old ideas;
Tensed against the wine-soaked washrag
Of the sky the trees erect themselves
In the last small oblivion of lights;
Talk grows animated . . . someone screams . . .
This passes, these days, for the Bohemian.
Still, the knees of two bright things
Are touching . . . Everyone's lost the theme:
What is the mind compared to it,
To feeling's theatre always in flames,
On the stage, its aging, ludicrous opera
Still faintly heard among the ruins?

The Long Island Night

Nothing as miserable has happened before.
The Long Island night has refused its moon.
La belle dame sans merci's next door.
The Prince of Darkness is on the phone.

Certain famous phrases of our time
Have taken on the glitter of poems,
Like "Catch me before I kill again,"
And "Why are you sitting in the dark alone?"

Rilke's Childhood

What angel woke
one morning in his blood
while he stood standing
in a childhood dream,
the lake of a mirror
in the bedroom before him?
Or at the breakfast table
saw in the cold milk
winter going by,
out the window a slow train
silently drawn across
a field of ice,
the suspended breath
of mourners in the air,
the ponds darkening
below a line of trees?

Elegy for My Sister

1

Getting out of bed one day, you broke
Your leg simply by standing up,
The bones too frail, the marrow gone,
Melted into a kind of eggshell sawdust,
The Crab, and chemotherapy against it,
The cure as killing as the pain it cured . . .

Why torture myself? Or you?—sailed into
The port of Nothing or that Elysium
Of childish happiness the heart sets store by,
Which, for you, would be a house in Larchmont,
Or the first time you arrived in Paris. . . .

2

Now the vials have closed and all the druggists
Vanished into smoke, along what walks
Will the ghost of you appear in a summer nightgown,
Silvery as moonlight on a sill,
Supple as the girl you were, who, frowning,
Dazzled guests with showy piano pieces?
You never got the hang of it, never quite took in
The Bach Partitas or the Chopin Études,
Languishing always over "Clair de Lune"—
Moony on the upstairs porch and downcast,
Waiting for the phone to ring, or waiting
Simply for the end of waiting. Left in
My possession—the irony of phrases!—
Is a photograph of you posed on a pony
Somewhere in Maine—white cap, white coat—
And one from Lakewood. I remember going
Up by train once, dancing in the aisles
While the train sneaked through faint zebra woods of
     pine. . . .

3
That afternoon will come when the schoolgirl walking
Home from the classroom in the spring will feel
The first onslaught of the terror of seasons,
The blood of the hour a permanent imprint.
Approaching the bridge, will she be in her newness
The last straw just as the ship in the river

Appears and the jaws of the bridge fly open—
The drab barge below with its scruffy captain
Commanding the air with bleatings and whistles,
The smokestack's blunt, swift-moving cigar
Blurring the trees in a smudge of smoke,
The birds in the sky in a net, then not?

Above the run-down, oily garages
Of the Bronx—old brickwork, carwash rinses,
The abandoned piecemeal junk of the car lots—
A vapor trail goes into the workshop
Of the clouds, the spring comes on in the bushes,
Forsythia making its annual statement.

The bridge underneath is ever so slightly
Tearing a suture of itself in secret;
And what is most feared is about to happen:
The stage-set of a world taken for granted
Will drop from the sky, robots of ashes
In clouds grow solidly real, and murders

That always before occurred at a distance
Strangle the neck at home. How the small thing
Matters: the phones getting through, the cables
Never exhaling invisible, lethal
Fumes, the macadam keeping its bubbles
Of tar intact. . . . The bridge sways, opens,

And the cell is about to distort the message
Life had meant it to carry from the start,
Letting death's emperor through. The tiny
Deadly protein blossoms. The blossoms
Open to yellow, true yellow in the spring
Outside your Memorial Hospital window.

4
What errors you made you made in wanting
To be warm again or held or human
And not for the wolf of cash or the mean,
Sloe-eyed beauty of power or the game
Of the wily outwitting the unaware,
Or simulated pain used as a lure.
How stupid the endings of life can be!
Old age not seeing the sea at its foot,
Not hearing the music still to be heard.
Dead to all things but the shape of the self,
The violent tear out blood with their hands,
The insane hold up the cardboard pieces
Of a world they can no longer fit together,
And the cruel: the slack nurse, the greedy aide,
The doctor no longer aware of pain . . .

5
How all the terminals of the body
Ply their invisible servings and turnings,
The loading of freight, the slipping of cargo

Into the cell, the interior vision
Blind as the blood erasing the causeway
Connecting vital island to island.

What are ideas but architecture
Taking nature to heart and sustaining
Inviolable forms: the fleur-de-lis,

The subtle acanthus, the shell-like dominions
Of diamond accretions royal on coal,
The Gothic tower and the rabbit warren,

The fine interchange of matter and matter,
The natural and social shifting in the bonds
Of dialogues and elegies that rise from soil.

6
All the allowable days on circling
Boats turning inward toward the center
Of the circle of the water of the river
Have been disallowed by the squarely arriving
Tugboat from which a peg-legged captain
Smoking a panatela is lowered
Into a launch behind him his shadowy
Crew and now you see them advancing
Climbing the ropes toward the deck you're on
The smoke the river the trees going past you
Into the mist the birds growing weaker
Downriver somewhere there is connected
Song water falling rapids of birdcalls
Way off the cry of the throat of fever
The faintest releases of animal sound
The sky coming nearer, closer and closer,
The distances moving toward you and farther
Away the repeated echoes of names
Called across water   then it is over.

Aspects of Lilac

By the turn of the driveway, two lilacs have called
Attention to themselves, not by an excess
Of bloom but by an attenuation
Of design: altered shadow on gravel.
Gone for good are those understated
Cases I rescued from worthless soil:
Ripped-off dusty miller from the beach,
Or, struck by overdoses of rain,
Spoiled spotted-leaf geranium. Worse
Is the thud of birds that kill themselves
By flinging their bodies with force against
Glass windows and doors as if this were
Some sort of morgue for feathered things.
The deaf and dumb would find all language
Futile here; nature is silent—
But underneath the silence, struggle.
While powder-puff clouds are showing off
Quickening shapes against more stately
Clouds behind them, an ant has dragged
A fly across the threshold, a mealy
Bug fastened its sticky jaws
Into the crotch of two green stems,
Chewing the asparagus fern to scruff.
Last night the moon had a Byzantine flare
Of lemon gold like the goldleaf halos
One sees in the early Italian masters—
Venice, in fact, comes to mind, the palazzos'
Sandcastle, ice-cream feats, effects
Childish but pleasing, of spun-stone heights,
While a rat stands gnawing a lettuce leaf
At the edge of one of the canals. And sex
Like a frog jumps onto the screen at once,
Its spiritual and degraded aspects
Equally keen. In fall, when the first
Earth colors harden and oak fire starts

Its flame and rust, memory dotes
On the old clichés of the unexpected.
Desire never knows the end of the book
Any more than the leaves of the lilac dug
Up in the woods, brought home, and planted
Can tell us whether its roots next spring
Will burst into purple or white cascades.

Four Birds

"Wake to the sun," the rooster croaked,
First bird of the day. The world, light-flecked,
Chiselled its lineaments into form.
Where was all that fine light coming from?

"Trance at the wonder," the second sang,
Whose five dry notes urged the ongoing
Afternoon on. "Why wake and stir?"
It asked. And asked. There was no answer.

"Live through the muddle." That from the next one.
Not very helpful. It looked like rain,
Or fog in the offing. Twilight. Then
It sang again from an oak or pine.

Silence. How I waited for the fourth!
Time was a negative dipped into its bath,
The dark a fixative that slowly made
For every windowpane its window shade.

No messages arrived. No music bared
The soul for its penitence. Up the stairs
No hint of a footfall. The night passed.
"Croak by your hand," said the crow at last.

Incomplete and Disputed Sonatas

1

After the plagues and the dispossessions,
Survival's one idea gives way
To ideas of civility:
Immigrants rise out of muddy shoes
Up to their sky-high penthouse suites,
A piano waxed to perfection wheels
On all three legs down a pine-needle path
Through woods. French windows reveal the sky,
And one sharp branch of forsythia
Sticks its yellow muzzle of a gun
Into the proper corner window,
Making the composition perfect.

2

Someone playing Schumann begins
To alter the prepared arrangements—
The idea of dissolution comes back again:
The needle's track runs backward in its grooves,
A window-cleaner like a flake of icing
Drops to the ground, the glass shatters,
Cutting badly on the way down.

3

Still,
You may see, curled up in still
Another window,
A girl intent on reading a novel,
Her hair suffused with sunlight blonder
Than she. Music by Mozart,
The G-Minor Quintet saying
How nothing lasts
But music by Mozart.

4
Are we approaching the coast?
Dark, you have given too many assignments.
Rain drums on the slattings of the deck.
Cold warns the room of its sudden menace.

5
Wagnerian sails
Go by the window—
Somewhere in fog a net and trident,
Neptune stranded on a tip of pine,
Appalled to be a god in a suburb.

6
Every day to wake to the world's work,
To take apart the watchwork of seasons,
Houses I cannot remember, palaces
Burning among the ghostly senators,
Or around a fire a circle of men,
The dogs with their wary eyes walking
Out of the forest to become domestic . . .
Tonight the storm's electrical transformers,
The purring abusiveness of cats in love.

7
Lately among apparently leafless
Trees I have had these afternoons
Of solitude and of loneliness,
As if I might die before I could tell
Those whom I loved that I had loved them,
As if when I woke I would slowly walk
To a bay window, look down, and see
Myself lying lifeless on gravel.

Impatiens

Your current pain no longer divides you
From the world of pain, bringing with it
Impatiens—pots of it, pink, red, white,
Plants glimpsed on a sill. Your pain
Lessens not by division but fattens
On earlier pain, those filaments and dredges
And tons of sand bottomed in a bag,
Sunsets staged in the curves of chairs,
Penitent clouds that do not argue
With the best intentions, and friends who desire
Both your health and the destruction of it,
Who love you, but love your pain as well.

There are those who have traced its trace on air;
Walking across their territories like kings,
They have sensed imperial gore somewhere,
Across the seas or beyond the mountains,
Staking out new sites, endlessly repeating
The warrior's success, colonies and tracts,
Landfalls, and even the ruin of grandeur
Beheld one night in an English dream.
Your pain is crossing the borders of patience,
Worse at night in a hospital room
Plastered with the cries of those who died there.

Your pain. It is intolerable. It is
Hardly, though, the anguish of the tortured
Beaten on cement, sleepless, raving,
Fingernails ripped out by skillful priests,
The grim surgeons who enjoy inflicting
The international instruments of torment,
The rack, restraints, electric currents,
Truncheons, all ready there for use,
For the vomit, urine, and feces of the cell.
So in all ways you are illustrated

And diminished, though you suffer at the sight
Of a small clay pot of thriving impatiens,
Pink, because it reminds you of someone,
A child waking up to the world's blight.

Standards

Sadly among the patient standards
Of trees the twirlers arrive to conduct
The last of the summer's orchestral pieces.
The garden's icetray of seeds is about
To swing back into its glacial room;
In less and less tree, in more and more shades,
Being is only a caster of rings,
A moment oiled by an Indian giver
Each year becoming more subtle in taking
Down the last partitions of leaves.

Across the field, in a field, some horses
Chomp on summer, green crop turning
Into a lawn of lap robes skillfully
Stitched, moss mounds thinning to moons
Of suède—so they appear from a distance.
The air is a brandy snifter of pine,
Fresh in this land of oaks and azaleas,
Of acid earth rhododendrons love,
A bit too sandy for roses but
Perfect for lilies that last a day.

The butterfly's parturition, its swift
Demise occur in a wink, and things
That took their own sweet time to be
Themselves reluctantly take their leave:
Seeds, weeds, the gods of the seasons
Bowing in mist, while in the wings
Two sets of actors are exchanging costumes,
The street urchins shaking hands with the angels,
The woods about to speak to the axeman.

Two times the light gets lacier: when
Insects pattern the leaves with bites,
A ferocious munching one hears at night

In spring—an invasion of gypsy moths—
And now, when the leaves are no longer partial
But slip away and are totally gone,
So though there is less and less of light,
Still, by being able to shine
Down through the vertical hallways of oaks,
It seems to increase in intensity.

The seeds with their little valises fly
Over the scene and look for a landing;
Any spot of common earth will do
In the sun. Preferably moist. The dew
Does wonders. Already one sees next year
Spring up: tree, flower, bush, and weed,
The butterfly conjoin with the tiger lily,
The roadside aster purple the border,
The process random, none of it wary,
Forgetting how dumb form is in history.

Ocean houses breaded with lilac,
A dry stick of a hut embedded in sand,
Things man-made and some things natural
Go: one storm slams through a solid
Wall, brings trees to their knees, and sucks
A beach house down from the dunes in boards;
The beach changes its contours nightly,
And so, if you are coming to see me,
Come soon. Today's astringent, perfect,
A perfection not to be known for long.

Stars

For James Merrill

In some versions of the universe the stars
Race through their orbits only to arrive
Back where they started from, like me planning to
Visit you in Greece—how many times?—I never have,
And so your house in Athens still remains
A distinct possibility, like one the stars
Foretell in the sky or spell out on the magic
Ouija board you use to bring to life,
Out of the night's metaphysical static,
Ephraim, that Greek, first-century Jew
Who telegraphs his witty messages to you,
The cup as pointer capturing alive
The shorthand of the occult, divinely comic . . .
But who's responsible for the result—
The spirit world or you?

    Do you as I do
Have to fend off Freud's family reunions:
Those quadraphonic old familiar quartets
Positioned nightly, bored, around the bed—
No speaking parts, and two of them at least
Certified deadheads? What does friendship mean
Unless it is unchanging, unlike Ovid's
Metamorphoses where everyone's becoming
Something else—Poor Echo and her voice!
And poor unlistening, unhinged Narcissus;
Poised above the water for the glassy foreplay,
He sees more than himself in the reflecting pool:
It's Algol, the ecliptic—a variable.

We met in the forties—hard to believe!
You were in uniform and I in mufti.
And went our separate ways: you to matinées
At the Opera and I to the City Ballet.
Though one extraordinary day, much later,

We heard "Wozzeck" at a dress rehearsal,
Sitting in the empty Met at 39th Street
In a center box—was it Mrs. Morgan's?
(How much more pertinent to this poem's theme
If it had belonged to Mrs. Astor!)
The nascent glitter of the oval boxes,
Brass railings sheathed in velvet, dimming lights
Preparing the round hush for music's entrance,
The subtle musk of perfumed dust, and dusky
Presences, now ghosts, floating round the room
(Now itself a ghost, long since torn down):
Old opera stars and their old audiences.
What a performance! Never interrupted
Once by—God!—was it Mitropoulos?
I think it was. Another Greek. You know
How memory fuzzes up the facts. But one
Odd fragment still remains. You brought along
A paper bag with chicken sandwiches
We ate out in the lobby in the intermissions,
And never was a sandwich so delicious—
Drunk on music, we staggered down the stairs
To daylight streaming in to air the lobby,
Surprised to see—beyond the doors—Broadway!

Loew's "Valencia" 's ceiling made of stars
Was not "The Starlight Roof"—that came later—
Starry-eyed, I watched the North Star rise
At Fire Island Pines. Below the equator,
I assumed it *fell*, and the Dipper, in reverse,
Spilled the velvet black back into darkness—
All wrong, of course. At the Planetarium,
Projected stars I craned my neck to see
Brought back the "Valencia" 's vaudeville to me,
A passion of my childhood: backbend writhers,
Lariat rope-skippers, and a stream of comic
Yodellers from Switzerland who did their stuff

Under twinkling stars. Like these above:
Calculating Leda floats above the hedges
To surprise The Swan nightly at his pool
Opal in the moonlight as he drinks his fill,
Galaxies flung at random in the till
Of the Great Cash Register the world comes down to;
When the drawer slams shut, a once and only
Big Bang Theory may be shot to hell,
And not again the great unknown designer
Fling into the firmament the shining things
Above a world grown ludicrous or tragic,
And our sick century may not recover:
The Spanish War. The Yellow Star. Vietnam.
Five . . . or is it ten by now? . . . assassinations.
The stars were crossed, the lifelines cut too soon—
And smaller fallings-off fall every day,
Worse for being seen against the view
Of the starlight's inexhaustible display,
Of which we cannot make out half the meaning . . .
Did Starbuck, on his watch, stare to starboard,
Gazing at the sea through meteoric showers,
And hear, above, the music of the spheres?
Or merely hear the watch bells chime the hours?

The Little Dipper in East Hampton dips
Above the pines, as if, at my fingertips,
Light so highly born could be borne down
From vibrancies that glisten and touch ground . . .
It brings the dawn, it brings the morning in.
I'm having coffee and reading your "Divine
Comedies." At "D": "*Dramatis Personae . . .*
Deren, Maya . . ." Maya and I once met
In Washington Square and talked for hours
Of images. Was film sheer poetry? Etcet.
Of "Meshes of the Afternoon," "At Land" . . .
I saw myself in both films recently . . .

How much I had forgot! My part's half cut . . .
I dazzled myself, though, just by being young.
And "Auden, Wystan," master star of all,
A major figure in the "Comedies,"
Poured wine for me at Cherry Grove and said
At least ten brilliant things too fast to hear—
Part wit, part stammer, part schoolboy pioneer,
His High Church, camp, austere "My dear,"
Soon switched into the beach vernacular.
I've found that conversations with the great
Are almost invariably second-rate,
Yet, when he died, I felt that truth had left
The world for good, its foremost spokesman gone.
You meet the characters in Proust at parties,
Dimly aware that you are one yourself
Fated to be translated badly like
A comedy of manners curried into Greek
With too many stars, none self-effacing,
Or worse, find yourself dressed for a Fable,
Lightly disguised as the Star of Ages . . .
Saying that, I feel the slightest pull . . .
How odd! I think I'm drifting . . . Lifted up
Past houses, trees . . . And going up and up . . .
You're rising, too, into the stellar soup . . .
Stop! Where's Newton! Where is *gravity?*

In observation cars, beneath balloons,
We falter, float into the atmosphere
Of Webster's Third . . . or is it the O.E.D.?—
Either is outer space for you and me—
And soar aloft among word constellations.
The stars are verbs; the nouns are novas; pale
Adjectives grow bold at our approach;
The sulphur schools of fish are lit, and flare;
Paper fire-cinders feather into blackness

Their ember-edged remains, and then, no matter;
From your little lip of balcony you fish
The icy wastes while I cast my line
Into the squirming lists. Out of the blackened blue,
Racing upward into the stratosphere,
The purest draft of crystal veers toward you.
We sidle up through drop-cloths rushing down,
Go zigzag, pause, and coasting on a calm,
Reach up to pluck the stars like words to make
A line, a phrase, a stanza, a whole poem.
A planet's surface blinds us; we look down:
Moonlight's aluminum coats the molten wells . . .
Is that a comma? Or a quarter moon?
One decimal of saturated gold,
A coin drops in its slot, and turns to ash.
You scud into a diamond bed ahead,
I drop toward burning coals that soon grow cool . . .
Exclamation marks against the sky,
Our hanging baskets periods below,
We sway, like ski-lifts hung from chains. The dark
Is filled with phosphorescent question marks.
In a snow shuttle, the Great Bear flies,
Angling for the Pole. How light his fur!
The Dog Star puts his solar collar on.
It's crystal-cold. One needs the inner darkness
Lit by spirit lamps or, like Aladdin's,
Rubbed to bring the genie, warmth, back home.
Stupendous flocks . . . Is it the world in flames?
Or just the Milky Way? Too late! Too late!
Again we rise up through the lit bazaars,
Punchdrunk, against the carbon, seeing stars.

From Rules of Sleep *(1984)*

In Umbria

For Daniel Lang

The wrong assumption flirted with the possible:
A grave burst open,
St. Clare's body still in her nightdress
Flying in a vertical rush to Heaven,
Abandoning the stones speechless with sadness.
At first the woods were level, then unreal,
The stars alarmed by a wind shift, moonlight
Startled by the thrill of the extraordinary.
But soon the unexpected settles down,
Settles down, becoming ordinary
In landscapes compelled to tell a story—
Landscapes like this one seen from the tilted
Courtyard in front of the church at Assisi,
The hills peaceful with their fuzzy greenery,
Angels at rest who ask no questions,
And a sky that sails, finally, serenely.

In the church's glassed-in reliquary
A saint's bones give off neither a peculiar
Shining nor any semblance of the human.
Help is coming in this hospital
Of souls where first-aid never arrived
On time before; the holy bandages
Being folded now by hands of mercy
Will let that woman in black rise up
From her wounded knees, that gnarled old man
Believe in the sanctity of the uninjured.

Happy the monks strayed out of history
Walking forward toward the central fountain,
Dry, ornamental, surrounded by grasses.
Only the play of light on the hills,
Captured for good in religious paintings,
Serves as an emblem of the spiritual life
Of Umbria: three syllables of shade—

Or one—cast by a cypress tree
Alone in a field whose brush of thin
Shadow works the sundial of the day;
In this fief of the godly, art
And feeling are as intertwined
As orthodoxy and heresy.

"Far" and "down" are being redefined
In a medieval town up in the mountains.
Which is farther away: the valley
Floor invisible below or the distant
Hillside glimpsed in a haze of ozone—
The horizontal and the vertical
Having lost all meaning? The circle thrives—
The semicircle, rather—of the mountain
From whose rim the houses stacked in stone
Rise up again; a church and fountain
Domesticate a fortress of a town
Where the *gelateria* stays open late
And the park has the charm of the unnecessary.

So civil is it all
That one might be at a luncheon party
Attended by monks in a sunlit courtyard,
Clerics explaining to Swedish tourists
The history of the single Tintoretto
That has kept this monastery alive
Three hundred years. The wood of crucifixion
Lies everywhere about; its subject is either
Bred in the bone, in Umbria, or nothing:
The flowers are heavy with theology,
The birds fly by like Biblical quotations.
In all this shadowy world of sunlight,
In tiers and tiers of arranged hillsides,

Rays of evening fall on the earthworks.
The shades of Umbria are growing darker.

And what the dead have to say today
Is old, old as the hills, a phrase
Meaningless until one stares at these
Great slants of grave sites, reaching up
Always to the light, which the dead can't do,
Whose every particular is shelled to bone;
They say, "Our hearts, too, were full
Of sunlight once. Joy is in the shade.
Look at it. Look. It is beautiful."

The Gallery Walk: Art and Nature

A lesson in perspective, a trick of light?
How to daub some innocent canvas
With the seedy grapeshot of a current fashion?
No, I am only trying to teach you
What pleasure is, and also about
The end of things,
And how the two of them go hand in hand.

To me, music is at the heart of it,
And painting of every kind and school,
From Florence's serene Annunciations—
Mary surprised, not astonished, at the news,
Some angel like a flat-footed bird nearby
Or threshing upward toward a thread of goldleaf,
Blue-green finicky, brushworked hills
Beyond—to Pollock's wounded linoleums
Wriggling away, or Rothko's bars
Of cathedral light. I am also partial
To the monumental:
Sculpture against the ruins of sculpture,
Afternoons in Rome, light everlasting.

Something, too, should be said for the crafts,
The ewers, crocks, cups and saucers
Spread out on tables over centuries
For the altar's royal elegants, or for
The crop dividers coming home at dusk
To share their simple grains and leaves.
Each time among them two figures appear,
Repentant Adam, unknowledgeable Eve,
Boring as ever with the family news,
And always there comes the same surprise:
She falls down in the middle of a joy,
He keels over at the wedding feast,

And then the lament goes on and on,
Witless, without humor, dumbfounded, grim . . .

And so it is better to look at the dancers,
Or these beautiful canvases of dancers dancing,
Or listen to music recreate the pulse
Of sounded, marvellous emotions caught
In the lines of the body, its grace and flights,
And to see on the wing of a violin
Nature soaring in, all green,
A tree, in which a bird will seek
Its habitation the summer long,
Singing its heart out, as usual.

Rome: The Night Before

I

On the terrace of the Villa Aurelia
Overlooking Rome (obscured by trees)
A form of life sprang into being
Too ideal to outlast the moment:
You sunbathing, reading in the sun,
And I flicking dead leaves and dried blooms
From geraniums in terracotta pots,
Each looking like a shrunk Napoleon.

We lived high up in Roman air, looked down
On a summer resort of corrugated stone,
Echo and rotunda, footfall, dome—
History turning corners everywhere
As if the faces of the night before,
Random visions of the street, were now
Individually fixed in marble brawn
Or in the cool shade, room on room,
In the Villa Farnesina or the Vatican Museum.

But museums in Rome are tautologies;
The same faces one sees hurrying past
On the streets are up on the walls and there-
Fore doubly visible: the seer and the seen,
With the same elegance at work—its fine
Italian hand springing from a fountain,
Or serving food and wine, its eyes and ears
Listening for birds down by the Tiber
Or watching, along with us, the ocular
Skylight dome of the Pantheon
Catching its round of sun or rain.

2

In the dowdy, magisterial squares
Of sculpture in Trastevere,
What generosities of light and water!
And everywhere the dirt lies underfoot
To prove the human imprint's never lost,
No, not even in the midst of grandeur.

3

How shall the cypress imagine the fuller
Shade of the beech, or the brain design
The once living architecture of the skull?
No watcher of water can bring that moment
In time alive when the first impression
Appears, a dent in marble, the erosion
Of stone by falling water, or the pressure
Of human weight, one plane worn down
A touch each century; a chemical
Film of cancer, working its way in,
Tears at the meat of statues and muddies
The finest Roman torso, Roman profile,
The dribbling-down distortions of the air
Turning a colossus into candle wax.

4

Everything permanent is due for a surprise,
The stopped stunned by the ever-changing.
What everybody always took for granted
Astonishes a second before it disappears,
Like the dinosaur who left a plate of bones
And was gone for good. In Rome one feels
Duration threatened day by day,
Not knowing which of its great works will last,
Flesh and marble the same mix of mortar.

Venice: Still Life

At one of the tourist traps in Venice,
Alone for lunch, I watch a guide's
Innocuous school of fish swim by,
Back up, swirl in, to nibble a bit,
Awash among the famous paintings
Before they head out for the icons—
Shrines whose outlines will dissolve in moonlight.

And where else have life and art become
So utterly as one that this not very good
Meal hastily set before me by a saint
With certain thuglike, endearing thumbs
Might be a still life for all the taste
It has, a still life by a second-rate
Dabbler over for the trade, or glass,

Or to study the artful glaze of still lifes
Hanging on a wall in the watery light
Spewed up from a canal at God knows what
Lucky hour of dispensation: a gleam,
Or a steady mirrorlike glint and flame,
The kind that twilight walks down steps for
Into the crowds of water at its feet.

Mentioning These Things

Mentioning these things: a clavichord cover
Closed, its gray-green plank fastened tight
By the scrolled Spanish clasp of two gold hinges,
Its chain a tether on the charms of the baroque;
Across the room a star-struck sprig
Of magnolia stuck in a jar of water—
A crystal shape of light, marred at the top
By pieces of bark that the cut branch sheds,
Scumming the surface with spent bits of life
(Husklike cups enclosing the blossoms
That dry out as they bloom, like those of cotton);
On the terrace two deck chairs seem to invite
The arrival of a painter who is strangely drawn
To another landscape—Chinese mountains, say,
Or a desert whose wildflowers are in bloom;
Since there is nothing here but waiting,
The sun is drawing trembling spider patterns
Of light on the rough yellow stucco of a wall,
In the room a fireplace swept of ashes,
Its hearth scoured clean by a stiff whisk broom,
And, at right angles to a rosewood chest,
A desk is waiting for its poems to light,
The glass door at a slant, the sky aswim
With the clouds and touches of the known unseen.

The Restaurant Window

A time-lapse camera might do it justice,
This street outside the restaurant window,
Feeling hurrying by on one side
And thought on the other.
Gradually night sponges up vision,
A moment so made up of other moments
No one can tell one famous variation
From another. Soon they will become the theme.
It is then that the power of form is felt
(Could it have been, all along, the subject matter?)
Connecting everything, the ginkgo's gesture
And the ginkgo, even permitting
The streetlamp turning on every evening
Its one small circle of illumination,
As if it were reading, over and over,
The same book of poems.

Insurgent sounds of music, bells
Add their bits to the pending structure,
A latent second holding in its spell
The chromatic shift to the second after,
Each table lamp an imitation
Of the light outside, and in the haze,
Part incandescence, part refraction,
Fine distinctions you have never grasped
Swim into view, the elusive becoming
A mute but embodied expectation.

And now as people vanish from the street
(A hurricane lamp outlasting its tempest)
The trees relax into Japanese silence;
Even the glasses assume their true property:
Waiting only to be filled or emptied.
The world's no more than a neutral surround
Until it begins to move with purpose—

Such moments are lived alone: at night
In the white capsule of a hospital room
After the warm visitors have left,
The chill of what is about to happen
Settles between you and a stranger
Walking into the room politely;
Both of you know you are not there for nothing.

Thus this street: it has an ending somewhere,
An event flaring out of sight in the west—
The sunset, already settling for less.

Fingerprints

Does the café table bear the fingerprints
Of Victor, his transmuted fires gone,
And one more vodka on the waiter's tray?
The trees here smell of zinc. The setting sun
Is dragging its copyright down the sky—
I'm at the bay where nothing ever happens.

And nothing brings back Sally. Nothing can.
Her second marriage doomed, that Indian giver,
Hope, took back the few small crumbs he gave her.
Taking her last shaky look at the river,
Dissolving Nembutal in gin, she swilled
The whole concoction down from a cocktail shaker . . .
Even forms of suicide go out of fashion.

Nikos? Who knows where former Greek gods go.
Into a pantheon out in the Hamptons?
When last seen, he was cadging drinks
At a tourist joint in Maine, then moved from there,
Became a bartender, and then a bar,
Drinking his way from harbor to harbor.

Leslie, if you should rise up from the deep,
Like a diver reversed in a sped-up movie,
Tell me, why did you leave us all for M.
And die beside him in a leaky cruiser
In foul-weather gear in Great South Bay
With a storm coming up, you the best sailor

The boatyard and the Coast Guard ever knew?
Maybe some wise bird passing over
In instinct's annual fall migration
Can fill in all the stories, give them meaning,
Send us a clue or sign we'll understand,
Fall in the leaves, the sky cold blue.

Rooftop

Rain, will there ever be enough
For the black-tarred roof
Desiring still to become a mirror,
Ever enough slickness of ice?
Today it felt
In the silvering of its underside
A faint image—someone walking
Across it shuddering to be defined,
But when it tried
To shine, the figure, if it was a figure,
Vanished, leaving the fire escape
Empty without its life of crime,
And so the roof waits for the first appearance
Of anything, even a cloud, the curved
Faraway Saracen moon to light
Its way through this
Long winter of loneliness.

2

If it could hold a star, if some
Summer chair now bare of canvas
Would lend the sure spareness of structure
To its moil of undistinguished blackness,
Then it would make its mark, almost
As famous as the moon.

3

Spring has come, it can tell from the way
The light is leaving the living room,
From the way the beginning is beginning again,
A welling up, then a slackening—
Can a thaw settle in to stay?
Today it knew it was right because

The first light shadow of a leaf was thrown
In exquisite scale across its skin.

4
Does the ice confer
Grace on the skater's heel, the wing
Of a bird become pure speed because
It rises against the motionless?
How the sky shows off its talismans
Enhancing the outline of each thing,
The way the heavens miraculously
Have turned the drabbest skyline tonight
Into the golden ramps of a city
Filled with the spectrum's crisps and chars,
As if some bare Egyptian whittled
A fine gorget to decorate the neck
Of the cat goddess, a net of blazing fire.

Rules of Sleep

In the sludge drawer of animals in arms,
Where the legs entwine to keep the body warm
Against the winter night, some cold seeps through—
It is the future: say, a square of stars
In the windowpane, suggesting the abstract
And large, or a sudden shift in position
That lets one body know the other's free to move
An inch away, and then a thousand miles,
And, after that, even intimacy
Is only another form of separation.

No Harm

No harm would walk in and sit down,
I thought, this fifth time trying on
The passionate gloves, the wary shoes,

A sea oblique in the window shades,
And a distant phonograph's music sound
From the next or the next-after-that apartment.

But harm was already gloved and shod
In my feeling for what was never there,
Or was there in some illusionary life

Of the past, its shadow and its substance.
Here, on a strange coast, the foggy mornings
Lift predictably each day at noon,

The colored lights of the nighttime garden
Weaken and go out, the lukewarm pool
Has nothing of the swift embracing hum

Of a good cold sea. The future's apparition
Is here with me. Come closer, closer,
So we can play our roles—human, ghostly.

The Miles Between

Ambassador of rain to the night snow,
Custodian of all the miles between,
Who brought the morning tray of light and shadow,
Emissary sun, editing each form,
Illusion's minister who prints the leaf,
Goldsmith of autumn, and you, greenhorn
Conjuror of shoreline and sea storm,

The past's long unforgotten amateur,
Tearstruck highbrow, touchy and extreme,
Reaching for the heights to climb but one,
Soulmate looking for a place to lie,
By the talented flow of Iceland's lava,
By darkness coming down on Hungary,
I swear that you and I will meet again.

Song from the Intensive Care Unit

The dawn takes twenty thousand years
To creep up to my windowsill.
I had two pills to calm my fears,
And for my pain the usual.

Terror, shame, who seeks you out
At the four corners of my room?
The razor teeth of what small mouth
Begin to nibble at my name?

The Light Put Out

For Charles Wright

1
Expected twilight in the flies and wings
Was slow to learn its lines, but once it did,

Nothing could stop the evening's performance,
Suggesting a hand had slipped from the lightboard,

And when the outlines of the trees grew faint,
The background of the outlines fainter still,

Pain, which grows more intense at nightfall,
Occupied its theatre once again—

A chain-link fence of oblate light
The pool kept shaking and repairing.

2
Blinking rapidly to gain once more
The bric-a-brac of the taken for granted—

That common delusion of the mad, or those
About to disappear from the general view—

Looking out from behind a piece
Of wrought-iron, medieval armor, and

Dropping clinkers every time I winked,
I began the phone calls out of the dark.

3
Is that you, Long John Silver, at last?
Dragging your booty across the sill,

A star behind you like a little, burned
Fried potato stuck to the sky?

Nothing will pry it loose. Not even
Soaking. A spatula. Or time.

It's gone, it's back, like a ping-pong ball
Riding on top of the words at a movie.

You know all about it, One-Patch Pirate,
Opening your treasure. Light! All light!

4
A candle-bearer comes with bits of moon
And scrapes the specks of wax into the river.

They float under the eyelid of the sky
Reflected back as clouds on the water.

The birds are trying to teach rocks to fly—
Ungainly students of the night mirror!

5
A veil netted with black dots falls,
Dropping in coals in oil, black wells,

Flies not to be whisked away.
The free-for-all of the night winks on

Somewhere in the distance, more heard than seen
From here—a peculiar shade or screen

Feeling its way to a kind of vision
Alternate as dusk which has no reason

Not to go on to a conclusion affecting
The diners on the terrace rising to go

As well as the stranded traveller several
States away who is leaving the coughing

Hump of a bad used car to get help.

Making a Bed

I know how to make a bed
While still lying in it, and
Slip out of an imaginary hole
As if I were squeezed out of a tube:
Tug, smooth—the bed is made.
And if resurrections are this easy,
Why then I believe in all of them:
Lazarus rising from his tomb,
Elijah at the vertical—
Though death, I think, has more than clever
Household hints in mind and wants
The bed made, once, and for good.

Upstate

Graceful every tuck of the hills
For a stretch until the lopsided barn,
Abandoned hayrick, and broken silo
Make clear once again that Paradise
Is a place that must be left behind.
But, oh, how the hand yearns to make tall
The toppled, how the imagination fashions
Blueprints of former and future perfections—
Weedless gardens where everything blooms
On time and nothing attacks new growth
For its own subsistence. But the eye wanders
From the large to the small, the mind takes in
Only a single slice at a time,
And soon some other natural, wayside
Beauty cancels out thought, and we
Are riding through real and imagined hills
We think will be there forever because
We will be there forever. Our bland

Partnership's ever renewable passions
Roll along with their threatening qualms,
Their long and short endowments of worry,
But, by and large, we work, like the farm
We stared at: green hacked out of hardpan,
Acres of vegetables set in rows,
Rib-swaying, ancient, rust horses calmly
Chewing their way through middle-sized grass,
Its hutches, workable fields, and porch,
On which, way back among the trees,
Someone is silently watching us pass.

New Hampshire

1

When the loons cry,
The night seems blacker,
The water deeper.

Across the shore:
An eyelash-charcoal
Fringe of pine trees.

2

The lake reflects
Indefinite pewter,

And intermittent thunder
Lets us know

The gods are arriving,
One valley over.

3

After the long
Melancholy of the fall,
One longs for the crisp
Brass shout of winter—

The blaze of firewood,
The window's spill
Of parlor lamplight
Across the snow.

4

Flaring like a match
Dropped in a dry patch,
One sunset tells
The spectrum's story.

See the last hunter's
Flashlight dim
As he hurries home
To his lighted window.

The Swimming Pool

Once in, this expensive rectangle
Of blue, not quite the Caribbean,
Clear as a filtered tropical-fish tank,
Made going to the beach a dead issue.

A bay crowned with a bridge, a pond
Dammed overnight couldn't be more stunned
Than this sandy hole suddenly marine
Whose constant hum of plumbing soothes

An Atlantic uncluttered by waves and freed
Of a lifelong addiction to salt. Low tides
Bubble away in respective skimmers
Constantly doling out chlorine. A cloud,

Reflected less than a fathom deep,
Is surprised by the American way of life:
"So *this* is gardening," it says to itself,
Admiring free-form tendencies—its own

Ability to be both lamb and lion.
You who will be a shade of nature soon,
Look up—the now felled trees swim by
Casting a shadow by their very absence,

Just as in the city the opposite occurs:
Acetylene torches tear up time
As one more girder is hammered into space,
Wounding the sky with yet another spire.

But here, on this delusive Côte d'Azur,
Something festive and childish has been added
To the scenery—a waterfront of sorts:
This Mediterranean in a matchbox,

Whose lanes are meant for short Olympic laps,
Promises crowds arriving for imagined
Meets, the deck alive with oohs and ahs,
A latticework of lights plying the surface,

And, compliments of small bodies of water,
Birds flying in from everywhere in droves,
The seeds of wild thyme in their beaks,
With credit ratings from all over.

Miami Beach

Was Nature always a snob,
Distributing shorefronts only to the rich?
The poor have come to the right conclusion.

The car lots are dangerous, boutiques have closed
In the cleancut shopping mall whose potted palms
Stand helplessly guarding smashed flower boxes,

As slowly expensive logos drift away;
Subversively dreaming of the cold, signs crumble;
The place has the effect of a dead casino.

Yet the sea repeats its fire drill,
The waves coming in as they were meant to come,
All hailing light, beachcombers, tourists, one

Canadian spinster on her towelled maple,
A lifeguard selling products for the sun—
Still more arrive to take those heat waves in.

If you're high up enough to witness it,
This city's saving grace is light on water,
The bay on one side, the ocean on the other,

Collins Avenue strung out on lights—
Blue neon, the sign language of Paris—
Seen from a terrace overlooking Bal Harbour,

Though this evening's tropical aroma
Is marred by a sad old man who stands regretting
His waistline before a men's shop window,

Watching a coastline glassily reflected
Take its revenge, the tides undermining
The palmed investments of the big hotels,

Breaking through the breastwork of the dunes,
Thundering in to where they used to be,
To lap at the imported Louis Quinze

Already stricken with the plague of mold
Shifting on deer feet in draperied lounges
(So far no one has noticed the ugly

Patch of dry rot under the sofa,
Not even the Cuban trained in mildew,
Trained to pronounce the "doll" in "dollar,"

Otherwise it sounds too much like "dolor").
How botched is Paradise, how gone for good
Old rock and beach, this gorgeous littoral

Of palms adoring the sun, and sea grape,
Oleander, and white jasmine blooming
Under the nursing home's blinded windows

Where the cardiacs and the sun-stroked blackouts
Wheel past the splash of a tropical-fish tank
Leading a murderous life of its own.

A watering hole abandoned by the young,
Either the old will take it over
Completely or South American money

Found its new capital: a *kitsch* Brasilia
Of pre-stressed concrete with its air-conditioned
Swiss bank branch, and a single restored

Art deco hotel for absentee landlords
Scanning the sea rehearsing endlessly
Its threatened drama never to be performed.

Morning Glory

For Lee Krasner

Its wrinkled foreskin, twisting open, opens
The silky membrane of a French umbrella;
Within the lighted tent of the corolla
A five-ribbed shape (starfish invention!)
Supports, at the sun's behest, by tension
The small filament plumb at the center.

How blue is blue, how deft the manufacture
Of nature to define a color in a flower,
Balloon, trumpeter, and mountain climber
Among green hearts diagonally placed
In a matching, alternately rising pattern
On the overreaching wire of a stem

Always trying to ensnare another,
A string, anything, as long as it's above—
Chicken wire, trellis, fence rail, nail—
As if transcendence were simply a matter
Of going up and up, and up until
There's no place left in the world to go.

Einstein's Bathrobe

I wove myself of many delicious strands
Of violet islands and sugar-balls of thread
So faintly green a small white check between
Balanced the field's wide lawn, a plaid
Gathering in loose folds shaped around him
Those Princeton mornings, slowly stage-lit, when
The dawn took the horizon by surprise
And from the marsh long, crayoned birds
Rose up, ravens, maybe crows, or raw-voiced,
Spiteful grackles with their clothespin legs,
Black-winged gossips rising out of mud
And clattering into sleep. They woke my master
While, in the dark, I waited, knowing
Sooner or later he'd reach for me
And, half asleep, wriggle into my arms.
Then it seemed a moonish, oblique light
Would gradually illuminate the room,
The world turn on its axis at a different slant,
The furniture a shipwreck, the floor askew,
And, in old slippers, he'd bumble down the stairs.
Genius is human and wants its coffee hot—
I remember mornings when he'd sit
For hours at breakfast, dawdling over notes,
Juice and toast at hand, the world awake
To spring, the smell of honeysuckle
Filling the kitchen. A silent man,
Silence became him most. How gently
He softened the edges of a guessed-at impact
So no one would keel over from the blow—
A blow like soft snow falling on a lamb.
He'd fly down from the heights to tie his shoes
And cross the seas to get a glass of milk,
Bismarck with a harp, who'd doff his hat
(As if he ever wore one!) and softly land
On nimble feet so not to startle. He walked

In grandeur much too visible to be seen—
And how many versions crawled out of the Press!
A small pre-Raphaelite with too much hair;
A Frankenstein of test tubes; a "refugee"—
A shaman full of secrets who could touch
Physics with a wand and body forth
The universe's baby wrapped in stars.
From signs Phoenicians scratched into the sand
With sticks he drew the contraries of space:
Whirlwind Nothing and Volume in its rage
Of matter racing to undermine itself,
And when the planets sang, why, he sang back
The lieder black holes secretly adore.

At tea at Mercer Street every afternoon
His manners went beyond civility,
Kindness not having anything to learn;
I was completely charmed. And fooled.
What a false view of the universe *I* had!
The horsehair sofa, the sagging chairs,
A fire roaring behind the firescreen—
Imagine thinking Princeton was the world!
Yet I wore prescience like a second skin:
When Greenwich and Palomar saw eye to eye,
Time and space having found their rabbi,
I felt the dawn's black augurs gather force,
As if I knew in the New Jersey night
The downcast sky that was to clamp on Europe,
That Asia had its future in my pocket.

Howard Moss

Howard Moss is the poetry editor of *The New Yorker*.
Before joining its staff in 1948, he was an instructor
of English at Vassar College. The author of twelve
books of poems and three books of criticism, *The Magic
Lantern of Marcel Proust, Writing Against Time*, and
Whatever Is Moving, he has also edited the poems of
Keats, the nonsense verse of Edward Lear, a
collection of short stories written by poets, *The
Poet's Story*, and *New York: Poems*, an anthology.
A play, *The Folding Green*, was first produced
by The Poets' Theatre in Cambridge, Massachusetts,
and then by The Playwrights' Unit in New York
City, and another work, *The Palace at 4 A. M.*,
was produced in the summer of 1972 at the John
Drew Theater in East Hampton, directed by
Edward Albee. In the same year, Moss received the
National Book Award for his *Selected Poems*. In 1974,
he published a book of satirical biographies, *Instant
Lives*, with drawings by Edward Gorey. Moss received
a grant in creative writing from The American Academy
and Institute of Arts and Letters in 1968 and was
elected to its membership in 1971. In 1983, he was the recipient
of a Brandeis University Creative Arts Citation in Poetry, and,
in 1984, a National Endowment for the Arts Award.